Conscience and Autonomy in Judaism

A Special Issue of The Journal of Psychology & Judaism

Edited by Rabbi Levi Meier

HUMAN SCIENCES PRESS, INC.
72 FIFTH AVENUE
NEW YORK, N.Y. 10011-8004

ISBN 089885-364-8

Copyright 1986 by Human Sciences Press
72 Fifth Avenue
New York, New York 10011

All rights reserved. No part of this work may be reproduced or utilized in any form or by any means, electronic or mechanical, including photocopying, microfilm, and recording, or by any information storage and retrieval system, without prior permission from the publisher in writing.

Printed in the United States of America.

JOURNAL OF psychology AND judaism

Volume 10, Number 2　　　　　　　　　　Fall/Winter 1986

Guest Editor's Perspective
Rabbi Levi Meier, Ph.D　　　　　　　　　57 [3]

Editor's Perspective
Reuven P. Bulka　　　　　　　　　　　　58 [4]

The Struggle of "Self" Within Judaism
Reuven P. Bulka　　　　　　　　　　　　59 [5]

Psycho-*Halakhic* Man of Conscience
Rabbi Levi Meier, Ph.D　　　　　　　　　73 [19]

Struggling With The Image of God
J. Marvin Spiegelman　　　　　　　　　100 [46]

THE JOURNAL OF PSYCHOLOGY AND JUDAISM is dedicated to exploring the relatio ship between psychology and Judaism and examines this relationship on both a clinical a philosophical level. The *Journal* publishes articles that are related to the spheres of psycholo and Judaism and have implications concerning the synthesis of the two areas. The *Journal* serv as a forum for discussion and development of integrated approaches to uniquely Jewish proble in the clinical and meta-clinical realms.

MANUSCRIPTS should be submitted in triplicate to the Editor, Dr. Reuven P. Bulka, *Journ of Psychology and Judaism,* 1747 Featherston Drive, Ottawa, Ontario, Canada. K1H 6F Manuscripts from Europe, Asia, Africa, and Australia, as well as ISRAEL, should be sent to t Overseas Editor, Dr. Moshe HaLevi Spero, 66 Shaulzon, #13, Har Nof, Jerusalem, Israel. Manuscri should be typed on one side of the page, double-spaced throughout, on 8½" x 11" paper. A marg of at least one inch should be left on all sides. A title page should contain the names of all auth and sufficient addresses. A biography of 50–75 words should be included, (academic degrees, prof sional interests, publications), along with a full face photograph. An abstract of no more than 1 words should accompany the manuscript. References should be listed following the style used the American Psychological Association Publications Manual, 3rd Edition (1983). Citations fr the *Bible, Talmud, Midrash, Maimonides, Shulchan Arukh,* etc. should be incorporated into t text in parentheses following the pertinent quote or statement. The reference should refer to t overall work, not the specific volume. Where possible, references should identify standard Engl translations of the aforementioned works. Further information concerning the preparation manuscripts can be obtained from the Editor.

SUBSCRIPTIONS are on an academic year basis: $26.00 per year. Institutional rates are $ Prices slightly higher outside the United States. **ADVERTISING** and subscription inquiries sho be made to: Human Sciences Press, 72 Fifth Avenue, N.Y., N.Y. 10011, (212) 243-6000.

INDEXED OR ABSTRACTED IN: Psychological Abstracts, Index to Jewish Periodicals, C rent Contents/Social and Behavioral Sciences, Religious and Theological Abstracts, Social Scienc Citation Index, Selected Lists of Table of Contents of Psychiatric Periodicals, Modern Langua Association International Bibliography, Guide to Social Science and Religion in Periodical Lite ture, and Pastoral Care and Counseling Abstracts.

PHOTOCOPYING: Authorization to photocopy items for internal or personal use, or the inter use of specific clients, is granted by Human Sciences Press for users registered with the Copyri Clearance Center (CCC) Transactional Reporting Service, provided that the base fee of $2.50 copy, plus $.20 per page is paid directly to CCC, 27 Congress St., Salem, MA 01970. For those ganizations that have been granted a photocopy license by CCC, a separate system of payment been arranged. The fee code for users of the Transactional Reporting Service is: ISSN 0700-9801 $2.50 + .20.

COPYRIGHT 1986 by Human Sciences Press, Inc. Published biannually in Fall/Winter a Spring/Summer. The Journal of Psychology and Judaism is a trademark of Human Sciences Pr Inc.

Guest Editor's Perspective

I want to thank Rabbi Reuven P. Bulka, Ph.D., for inviting me to serve as the guest editor for this special issue of the Journal of Psychology and Judaism which is entitled *Conscience and Autonomy Within Judaism*. This special issue, like three previous special issues of this journal, constitutes a complete book. This book is based on the first Los Angeles conference on *Psychology and Judaism,* sponsored by the Chaplaincy Department of Cedars-Sinai Medical Center.

Rabbi Reuven P. Bulka, Ph.D., the distinguished editor of the Journal of Psychology and Judaism, focuses on the "Struggle of 'Self' Within Judaism." He delineates precisely where there is room for 'self' in Judaism which espouses the actualization of God's will as the ultimate goal.

J. Marvin Spiegelman, Ph.D., writes on "Struggling with the Image of God," from a Jungian perspective. He shows that conscience allows for every one's wrestling with the direct experience of the Divinity.

The last paper introduces a new approach toward integrating Psychology and Judaism. In this paper, entitled "The Psycho-*Halakhic* Man of Conscience," I demonstrate the centrality of conscience within Jewish law and thought. Furthermore, this approach allows one's subjective experience of life to emerge within the rubric of Jewish laws and customs.

These papers present an exciting beginning in delving into integrating the subjective experience of self within the framework of Judaism.

I, as guest editor, have not changed substantially any of the articles in this journal. At times I have made minor alterations for the purposes of clarity and consistency. I hope that I have not violated the contributions of the authors and assume complete responsibility for my changes.

Rabbi Levi Meier, Ph.D.
Guest Editor

Editor's Perspective

A number of months ago, at the initiative of Dr. Levi Meier, a member of this journal's editorial board, the first Psychology-Judaism Conference was held, in Los Angeles, California.

This was the first such conference held under the auspices of the Chaplaincy Department of the Cedars-Sinai Medical Center. In conjunction with the Center for the Study of Psychology and Judaism the conference proceedings are presented.

The first all-day conference took place before a packed house, and augurs well for the future development of the Psychology-Judaism dialogue.

I have asked Dr. Meier to act as guest editor for this issue of the journal, which contains the proceedings from that conference. We hope to publish, from year to year, the conference proceedings.

I am grateful to Dr. Meier for this bold and energetic initiative, as I am sure are all readers of this journal.

Dr. Reuven P. Bulka
Editor

The Struggle of "Self" Within Judaism

REUVEN P. BULKA received his Ph.D. from the University of Ottawa in 1971 and is presently the Rabbi of Congregation Machzikei Hadas in Ottawa. A member of the editorial board of Tradition, The International Forum for Logotherapy, the Journal of Religion and Health, and Pastoral Psychology, Dr. Bulka is the Chairman of the Family and Marriage Committee of the Rabbinical Council of America and Editor of its "Family and Marriage Newsletter." He is the founding editor of the Journal of Psychology and Judaism and has contributed many articles to various scholarly publications on diverse topics; he is also the author of The Quest for Ultimate Meaning: Principles and Applications of Logotherapy, The Coming Cataclysm: The Orthodox Reform Rift and the Future of the Jewish People, and Jewish Marriage: A Halakhic Ethic, among others.

ABSTRACT: A cursory discussion of the concept of self within contemporary society is presented. Some reasons for the present trends are suggested, and the implications of these trends are weighed. In the background of this analysis, some Judaic notions related to the concept of self are projected. Awareness of self, appreciation of self, affirmation of self, and glorification of self are conceptualized in a Judaic context. The thrust of Jewish law, and the place of the individual relative to the law, are further clarified.

It is generally assumed that one of the correlates of the maturation process is the developing consciousness of the self. A very young child does not think, in a detached manner, of the self. As one enters into the early teens, the concept of self begins to evolve. One is able to step outside of one's own body to look at one's self in a detached manner, and critically analyze the behavior of that self.

Of course, on the other end of the spectrum, truncated maturity is evidenced in individuals who only think in terms of the self, and do not go beyond. There is even a word in the English language which aptly defines such individuals. That word is self-ish.

The other side of selfishness is selflessness. In selflessness in its pure form, the individual does not think at all about the self, and is totally immersed in other individuals or in causes, or in a combination of the two.

Pure selfishness and pure selflessness are extremes which are not part of the real world. However, one could say that, in general, individuals within the human species are characterized by precisely what position they occupy on the wide spectrum between selfishness and selflessness.

In the contemporary arena, the preoccupation with the self is a ubiquitous feature of American society. By the late seventies, it was shown that seventy two percent of Americans spent a great deal of time thinking about themselves and about their inner lives (Yankelovich, 1982, p.3). The so-called rage for self-fulfillment has spread to virtually the entire United States population.

This quest, according to some, is inevitably a creature of its times, which borrows forms of expression from whatever convenient sources are available (Yankelovich, 1982, p.231).

In spanning much of the psychological literature of contemporary currency, the notion of self-fulfillment is a major theme. Nathaniel Branden, for example, speaks about the four concepts that are central to his work: 1) self-awareness; 2) self-responsibility; 3) self-assertiveness; and 4) self-acceptance.

He explains self-awareness as referring to the awareness of feelings, needs, desires, emotions, ideas, evaluations, and behavior. Self-acceptance is the acceptance of all these items and of the fact that these feelings, ideas, and behaviors are expressions of the self at the time they occur.

Self-responsibility is responsibility for being the cause of one's own choices and one's own acts, more along the lines of recognizing that the self is the primary causal agent in one's behavior, and that one accepts the responsibility for one's existence. Self-assertiveness refers to the assertiveness of one's desires, judgments, needs; one's right to exist and to be happy. For Branden, these four concepts are the foundation of morality (Branden, 1974, pp. 155–156). A more radical form of this notion underlines EST (Erhart Seminar Training). That school of thought goes so far as to assert that the sole purpose of life is to acknowledge that the individual is the source, and then the individual should choose to be what the individual knows the self to be (cited in Vitz, 1983, p.33).

Without attempting to justify this philosophy, one can perhaps see in it an equal and opposite reaction to the perceived imposition by religion on the human species. Religion ascribed all goodness to God; the human being without God was sinful, even evil. But evil, guilt, sin and neurosis have all been placed into disrepute by psychology, which sees all of these as detrimental to human health.

The equal and opposite reaction has been to say that all good emanates from within the human being. The human being is now the god who chooses, and whatever the human being chooses is right because it expresses the human self.

Obviously, neither extreme, the extreme of seeing the human being as evil in relationship to God, or seeing the human being as god incarnate, expresses authentic Jewish tradition. However, within the American societal context, there is a subconscious perception that religion denies the self; in defiance and rebellion against this trend the self is now being affirmed in its totality, and in extremes.

One interesting outgrowth of this focus on the self is reflected in the changing American attitude to marriage. In the late fifties, a survey of Americans showed that eighty percent were extremely critical of anyone who was in a single state, and stigmatized such individuals as "sick," "neurotic" or "immoral." The other twenty percent ventured no opinion. Only less than one percent had anything positive to say about the unmarried state.

However, by the late 1970's, the country's attitude to the single state had made a dramatic shift. From eighty percent who had previously condemned the single state, now only twenty five percent condemned the single state. Approximately sixty one percent were neutral on the matter, and a full fourteen percent looked upon the unmarried state as a legitimate and positive way of life. So, in the space of a few decades, single status swung all the way from being sick, neurotic or immoral, to a state which was not condemned, and certainly much more accepted and acceptable (Yankelovich, 1982, p. 95).

One may conjecture that what is at work in this dramatic change of opinion is the notion of selfhood. If the single state is what the individual desires, then no one has any right to criticize such a state. If it is, for that individual, the thing to do, then so be it. In other words, values have become more oriented around the self, and as a result, attitudes to marriage have changed accordingly.

Another interesting consequence of this striving for self-realization is reflected in the observation of a noted sociologist that self-realization is directly implicated in the spiralling rate of divorce in Western society. Americans seem to cherish the right to the unimpeded pursuit of happiness, no matter how much agony that pursuit may cause. In the several instances in which the pursuit of self-realization did not itself produce a separation, it nevertheless seemed to have contributed to marital strife (Weiss, 1975, pp. 8–10).

In other words, the rush to self-actualization, self-realization or self-fulfillment, however one chooses to label this penchant, has probably been the cause of as much grief as it has been the cause of satisfaction. Witness the fact that seventy percent of Americans acknowledge that even though they have many aquaintances, they have very few close friends, and they feel that this is a serious void in their lives (Yankelovich, 1982, p. 248).

Considering that the same percentage of Americans are bent on self-fulfillment, the friendlessness of American society would seem to be directly related to the quest for self-realization. The "looking out for number one," "the sky is the limit," the "how to be your own best friend" syndrome, the me first, or me only, or "all my desires must be satisfied" attitudes, obviously lead to relationships which are self serving, perfunctory, transitory, and by definition unsatisfying.

In an otherwise insightful analysis of the American situation, Daniel Yankelovich seems to place much of the blame for the focus on self at the doorstep of Abraham Maslow. He sees Maslow as having the unfortunate genius to combine in one theory, "the two massive defects of the self-fulfillment strategy; the idea of the self as an aggregate of inner needs, and the concept of a hierarchy of being that makes economic security a precondition to satisfying the human spirit" (1982, p. 241).

This is slightly unfair on two counts. Firstly, Maslow was not the only one to espouse this approach, and though he may have been influential, it is slightly absurd to link the self-fullfillment quest of seventy two percent of Americans to Maslow's theories. Secondly, Maslow himself seems to have retracted from the emphasis on individual self-fulfillment. He asserted, somewhat later, that "basic human needs can be fulfilled *only* by and through other human beings, i.e., society" (Maslow, 1971, p. xiii).

To some, it may not be satisfactory to speak in terms of society as the "requisite" for the fulfillment of human needs. Once again, what seems to be a fundamental value is reduced to need fulfillment. Nevertheless, the statement, and Maslow's subsequent amplification of the idea implicit in the statement, point very clearly away from infatuation with the self, and towards the necessity of integration with society in a meaningful way.

Yankelovich, after describing the dangerous path that America is taking, argues convincingly for an "ethic of commitment." He argues against the assumption that the more one's desires are filled the better, and that the pursuit of that desire is morally worthy.

Instead, the self is more than the sum of one's desires; self-fulfillment "requires commitments that endure over long periods of time . . . the expressive and sacred can only be realized through a web of shared meanings that transcend the self conceived as an isolated physical object" (1982, p. 254).

Yankelovich asserts quite forcibly that "By concentrating day and night on your feelings, potentials, needs, wants and desires, and by learning to assert them more freely, you do not become a freer, more spontaneous, more creative self; you become a narrower, more self-centered, more isolated one. You do not grow, you shrink" (1982, p. 239).

What Yankelovich said in the early 1980's, was long ago stressed by Viktor Frankl, not so much on moral grounds as on practical grounds.

Frankl claimed that

> the real aim of human existence cannot be found in what is called self-actualization. Human existence is essentially self-transcendence rather than self-actualization. Self-actualization is not a possible aim at all, for the simple reason that the more a man would strive for it, the more he would miss it. For only to the extent to which man commits himself to the fulfillment of his life's meaning, to this extent he also actualizes himself. In other words, self-actualization cannot be attained if it is made an end in itself, but only as a side effect of self-transcendence (Frankl, 1963, p. 175).

Frankl, already in the early 1960's, was able to pinpoint, in practical terms, the Achilles' heel in the self-fulfillment philosophy. The fact that Yankelovich was obliged to repeat, in his own terminology, Frankl's original warning, merely indicates that society was unfortunately oblivious to Frankl's observations. One hopes that at the very least, Yankelovich's warnings will awaken society to the consequences of its actions.

This rather lengthy preamble is a useful starting point from which to investigate the "struggle of self" within the Judaic context. It is recognized that the struggle of self is a preoccupation of a majority of the population. At the same time, it is recognized that such preoccupation, by its nature, limits human potential, and from a Judaic and societal perspective is potentially dangerous.

Maslow, in developing his hierarchy of needs, speaks of the need for self-actualization, which according to him, refers to "man's desire for self-fulfillment, namely, to the tendency for him to become actualized in what he is potentially. This tendency might be phrased as the desire to become more and more what one idiosyncratically is, to become everything that one is capable of becoming" (Maslow, 1970, p. 46).

Maslow seems to equate these two goals, namely to become what one idiosyncratically is, and to become what one is capable of becoming. However, these seem to be two different goals. The self-fulfillment promoters would like to philosophically equate the two, but there is a dramatic difference between becoming what one idiosyncratically is, and becoming what one is capable of being. The former speaks of having everything that is inside the system come out; the latter speaks of striving to transcend the self, and to reach beyond what one is.

With this in mind, a preliminary look at some basic components of the self within Judaism may be undertaken. Briefly, it would be useful to explore the Judaic position on 1) awareness of self; 2) appreciation of self; 3) affirmation of self; and 4) glorification of self.

Insofar as *awareness of self* is concerned, there are those who may espouse the notion of the human being's nothingness, that the self should be totally denied. One can say categorically that this does not represent mainstream Judaism. At the very best, it may be seen as an extreme to counter the equal and opposite extreme of self-glorification.

In the middle, which is where Judaism thrives (Maimonides, *Mishnah Torah*, Laws of Opinions, 1:4), awareness of the self is a basic requisite for life. This is best encapsuled in Hillel's famous rhetorical question, "If I am not for me, who will be for me?" (Talmud, Abot, 1:14). The answer is obvious, namely no one. Each individual has a sacred obligation to take care of the self and to address personal needs in a responsible fashion.

The obligation to care for one's self is accentuated in the Bible through the imperative; "Be exceedingly heedful of your selves . ." (Deuteronomy, 4:15). In other commandments, one is asked merely to observe. With regard to self-preservation, one is obliged to be *exceedingly heedful*. And it cannot be any other way. Since Judaism clearly espouses the notion of the human being as God's creation, one has no right to be derelict in the care that is extended to the self. Such dereliction is morally and theologically irresponsible.

Of course, as will be developed later on, meaningful life extends beyond awareness of the self and responsibility to the self, and enters into the sphere of transcending values.

The notion of *appreciation of self* implies having a positive self image. This is best expressed in the exhortation, "do not consider yourself as wicked" (Talmud, Abot, 2:18). Obviously, an individual who considers the self as wicked will, more likely than not, engage in self-fulfilling prophecy. This may express itself either in objectionable behavior, or in the failure to elicit the virtuous parts of the self. The individual who sees the self as wicked is likely to give up on the self, and not push the self to its limits.

A more well known principle within Judaism, "love your neighbor as yourself . . ." (Leviticus, 19:18), is also rooted in a positive appreciation of the self. This Biblical charge, which is considered an encompassing principle in the Judaic lifestyle (Jerusalem Talmud, Nedarim 9:4), equates the love that we should have of others with the love that we should have of our own selves. Evidently, an individual who is sour on the self will project accordingly in the encounter with others.

If an individual is to approach the dialectical encounter with others in a positive and accepting manner, then that individual must have a positive attitude towards the self, even a love and appreciation of the self. Through that love and appreciation of the self, one can then extend one's self, affirmatively and positively, to others.

This combined positive approach to awareness of self and appreciation of self leads to the third component in the discussion of self within Judaic tradition, namely *affirmation of self*. One of the dangers in espousing the current notion of the affirmation of self is that such self-expression may actually bring out the more obnoxious and distasteful components of the self.

Many a counselor has undoubtedly encountered the situation of an individual who, when confronted with a particular behavior pattern, be it cynicism, sarcasm, temperamental outbursts, or other types of insensitivity, and asked to explain why he or she engages in such behavior, will simply respond, "that's me." It is as if the individual is doomed to this type of behavior, since it is an expression of what the individual really is. This type of rationalization can quite possibly justify the most pernicious of abuses.

Within Judaic tradition, therefore, it would be impossible to countenance individual self-expression which goes to such an extent. Being that there are prescribed norms of behavior within Judaism, any affirmation of the self which runs contrary to these norms would not be justified. The strong individual is not the one who has the "courage to express the self;" instead the strong one is the one who is able to "conquer the innate desires" (Talmud, Abot, 4:1).

It is recognized that each individual has desires of one form or another, but that these desires, expressed in an uncontrolled manner, are harmful to the self and usually harmful to others. The strong individual is the individual who is able to conquer these desires. Judaic tradition does not ask the individual to deny and squash desire; instead the individual is asked to conquer the desire and to channel that desire into a proper expression, much the same way as a conquered army must follow the directives of the victorious forces.

The passionate urge for sensual expression is not, by its very nature, evil. In fact, Judaism views this desire as an absolute necessity if love and procreation are to be possible (Midrash, Genesis, Rabbah, 9:7). However, that passionate urge must be subordinated to the wishes and desires of the partner in such passionate expression. An individual who forces the self on the other because of uncontrolled desire engages in a form of rape. True love involves ensuring that the other is not merely willing, but also eager and equally desirous for the love expression. Strength in this regard demands control, and may in certain situations even call for temporary renunciation.

There is a continual wrestling with the individual's innate desires. The individual is urged to overcome these instinctual expressions with a heavy dose of *yetzer tov* (Talmud, Berakhot, 5a), which can be best explained as the proclivity for actualizing the good. The individual has two potentialities operating from within; the potentiality to express virtuous behavior, and to express instinctual desire, that which is labelled the *yetzer harah*. Yetzer harah is often wrongly interpreted as the evil desire, but desire on its own is not necessarily evil. The term *yetzer harah* is more correctly translated as the instinctual desire. It may become evil if it is left to its own devices and allowed to express itself in an uncontrolled manner.

Thus, in this continual wrestling within the individual between the differing potentialities, the hope is that the tendency towards virtuous behavior will outweigh and overpower the instinctual desires, and channel those desires in a positive direction. Judaic tradition affirms that the individual who is greater than another has a stronger instinctual desire, but has fought to overcome that desire and to channel it properly (Talmud, Sukkah, 52a).

One of the major conduits for identity, or self-affirmation, is through work. One's vocation or profession is closely linked to one's concept of self, and one's image of self. The importance of this link is perhaps most manifest in the absence of work, in unemployment. Many unemployed suffer from "unemployment neurosis," from the empty feeling, the void and vacuum for lack of work. Individuals who are unemployed often feel depressed, down on themselves, of diminished importance.

All this is reflected in a most insightful Rabbinic interpretation of the Biblical charge, "choose life . . ." (Deuteronomy, 30:19). *Choose life* is seen as referring to a profession (Jerusalem Talmud, Kiddushin, 1:7). A person who has a profession has a vehicle for livelihood, a reasonably assured pipeline of sustenance. Even more so this livelihood gives the person a sense of self-worth. "When you eat from the sweat of your hand, happy are you . . ." (Psalms, 128:2). There is a special and satisfying feeling when one eats from one's own efforts, rather than being dependent on the goodness of others.

This was apparently recognized by no less an authority of the human psyche than God. The first human, Adam, did not taste any food until after he had done some work (Abot D'Rabbe Natan, 11:1). God could assuredly have given Adam some food without making him work. The sustenance was available. But God understood that Adam would have a much better feeling for his food if he felt that he had earned it. And thus it is with the totality of life. Individuals generally desire a connectedness to life, a sense they are making a contribution, if they are to feel positively about themselves and about the world in which they live.

The notion of the affirmation of the self, or self-actualization, thus has some currency within Judaism, but it is a currency which operates within a specific context. It is in the context of subordinating one component of individual fulfillment towards a more ennobled human potentiality. Additionally, all this is directed towards the actualization of the transcending values that are the governing guidelines of Judaic lifestyle.

Individual self-expression is also secondary to another notion, the notion of community. The obligation which rests on each individual not to separate from the community (Talmud, Abot, 4:7), is another distinct limitation on unbounded self-expression. No society can survive as a society if it is merely a conglomerate of individuals who do whatever they please. Even such simple matters as stopping at traffic signals, which may often stifle the individual urge to get to one's destination as quickly as possible, are essential if society is not to destroy itself in its oblivion to oncoming traffic.

In the Judaic context, the notion of community is vital, not merely for survival, but for viable growth. The norms that an individual is obliged to adhere to on a personal level are also communal constructs.

Quite often, the individual, in consideration of communal concerns, will forego a personal desire. However, on balance it may be argued that whatever the individual may lose for the sake of community, is more than compensated for by what the individual gains from being part of a greater community.

Finally, in this cursory discussion of the notion of self within Judaism, it is useful to understand the notion of *glorification of self.* One must be aware of the self, and appreciate the self in a positive manner. Additionally, one should strive to affirm the self through actualizing one's positive potential.

All this, however, does not legitimize what may be termed the glorification of the self. In Talmudic terms, self-glorification is often referrred to as boastfulness. In its positive affirmation, we are asked to be of humble spirit; not just of humble spirit, but very, very, humble (Talmud, Abot, 4:4). The accent on extreme humility for the individual may be seen as the Talmudic check on uncontrolled self-expression. The self is good, the self is important, but the self is not everything. The self only works within a specific context, and is urged to see the self in a humble manner.

Humility does not mean thinking of the self as nothing. Such an approach breeds a negativity which creates problems of its own. The individual is instead asked to have a balanced approach to the self, to realistically see the self as part of a totality, and to subordinate to higher values. Self-satisfaction and boastfulness about past achievements only serve to obstruct the possibilities for future fulfillment. Thus, an individual who is boastful is considered to be defective (Talmud, Megillah, 29a), and haughtiness is equated with idolatry (Talmud, Sotah, 4b).

The obligation to honor one's parents is an area where the individual's quest for identity, and affirmation of self, might meet with some obstacles. The Talmud, in expounding on the obligation of children to honor their parents even after the parent's death, gives an example to illustrate this. If an individual is in a place where a request is likely to be heeded if the parent's name is invoked, that individual should not ask that whatever is done should be done for his or her own sake. Instead, one should defer to the parent, and ask that it be done for the parent's sake (Talmud, Kiddushin, 31b).

An individual in such instance may be inclined to affirm his or her autonomy, and insist that the request be honored on the basis of the individual's station within the community. However, since this is an opportunity to accord honor to the parent, the child is asked to forego identity affirmation and instead use the opportunity to accord honor to the parents.

This Talmudic dictate probably relates to the category of glorification of the self. In the face of the reality that one's existence is due to one's parents, one is asked, in humble recognition of this obvious fact, to acknowledge it throughout one's entire life. The respectfulness of the past that has made the present possible is a fundamental component of the Judaic lifestyle. There is more than ample room for the expression of the self within the context of Judaic values, but the expression of self should not be achieved by stepping on, or ignoring, one's parents. This is fundamental to the development of a coherent, respectful, and value infused society. It may not excite the gurus of self-fulfillment, but then again, these gurus are leading the public on a dangerous path.

The ultimate value within Judaism, as expressed in the Talmud, appears to be that "In all your ways know God" (Talmud, Berakhot, 63a). This is the all encompassing theme of the Judaic behavior pattern. The individual is asked to exhibit Godly behavior and emulate God in all of one's pursuits. This involves the exercise of compassion, kindness, and concern, and the showing of empathy to others, among other expressions. To do God's will as if it were your own (Talmud, Abot, 2:4), expresses the most noble form of value integration within the Judaic context.

The question which arises out of this conceptualization is—where precisely is there room for the self, in a faith expression which espouses the actualizing of God's will as the ultimate? Must one totally deny the self? Must one give the self over in totality to God? In other words, the question that is raised here relates to the matter of what precisely is entailed in the obligation to actualize commands. Is there room for the individual, and individual self-expression within such a system, or does such a system totally negate individuality?

> A short while ago I bought a popular Jewish tape for my young children. It contained this surprising dialogue. "Did you do a mitzvah today? Yes, I did a mitzvah today, I kissed my bubby (Grandmother). You kissed your bubby! This is not a mitzvah. It is a nice thing to kiss your bubby, but it is not a mitzvah. If you kiss a mezuzah (parchment on a doorpost), that is a mitzvah."

These lyrics reflect most pointedly one of the more salient distortions involved in the concept of mitzvah, or commandment. Since a mezuzah is discussed in the Bible, but a bubby, or grandmother, is not, it is immediately assumed that the kissing of a mezuzah is a fulfillment of a Divine commandment, whereas the kissing of a grandmother is not. However, the Biblical obligation is to place a parchment scroll on the doorpost, which is the mezuzah (Deuteronomy, 6:9). No where in the Bible is it mentioned that one must kiss the mezuzah. On the other hand, the Biblical obligation to honor one's parents extends back to the obligation to also honor one's grandparents (Karo, Shulhan Arukh, Yoreh Deah, 240:24). Honoring the grandparents, in any way, shape, or form, is a fulfillment of a Divine dictate. Thus, the lyrics were a total misrepresentation of fact.

In actuality, one can posit that any human expression which works within the parameters of Biblical command is a worthy action. The Bible does not command that one should kiss one's parents or one's grandparents, but such obvious show of affection, which indicates devotion to and appreciation of one's parents or grandparents, is a worthy deed. At the same time, it is an individualistic expression. One does not go about kissing because one is commanded to do so. More likely it is a spontaneous show of affection which is genuinely felt. But precisely because it is spontaneous and genuinely felt it is a greater fulfillment. In other words, the place of the individual within the context of Jewish law is quite prominent, even necessary.

There is more to the understanding of the position of the individual in Jewish law. This concerns the conception of the law as the ultimate rather than as a means to an end.

Judaism was condemned by Immanuel Kant as a religion which fails to inculcate the inner appropriateness of morals, and instead demands external obedience to statutes and laws. Seeing the perfunctory behavior of some might incline many to agree with Kant. The argument is not so much with what one may see expressed, as much as with what the law is intended to be. Martin Buber refused to see revelation as a formulation of law.

> It is only through man in his self-contradiction that revelation becomes legislation. This is the fact of man. I cannot admit the law transformed by man into the realm of my will, if I am to hold myself ready as well for the unmediated word of God directed to a specific hour of life (Rosenzweig, 1950, p. 111).

For Buber, revelation was a contradiction of individual spontaneity. The two simply cannot exist side by side. In the formulations of both Kant and Buber, the law, rather than affirming the individual, represses personal development and precludes spontaneous reaction to the Divine call, perhaps reducing the human being to a halakhically programmed computer. But for Judaism "sheer compliance with the law as such was never regarded as the ultimate value, it rather represented a means to the fulfillment of the Divine Will" (Wurzburger, in Appel, 1970, p.8).

The two branches of Jewish law, the social legislation, commonly referred to as *bayn adam lahavero*—between the individual and his/her neighbor, and ritual law, or what is commonly referred to as *bayn adam laMakom*, between the individual and God, further reflect the nature and intent of Jewish law.

In the domain of social legislation, one quite frequently encounters the notion of *lifnim meshurat hadin* (Talmud, Berakhot 7a; Ketubot, 97a; Baba Kamma, 99b–100a; Baba Mezia, 24b, 30b), erroneously translated as "beyond the requirement of the law." The word lifnim actually means inside or within, so that the translation of this phrase should be "within the boundary of the law."

This suggests that insofar as social legislation is concerned, the law itself is not the ultimate. It is instead the lower, irreducible limit, the boundary line. Within the line of the law the human being oscillates between straddling the border and approaching the core, the heart and soul of the law. In straddling the border there is a danger that one may overstep, as well as a danger that the law may become a veneer which is used to camouflage personal interests. The notion of *lifnim*, or within, is thus expressive of a fundamental notion with regard to law, namely that the law is the border and that individual expression takes place within that border.

God's word can only go so far. After that it is up to the human being to take up the baton, to give to the body of laws meaningfulness and life with one's heart and soul. This is where enforceable Judaism ends and responsive and responsible human beings enter.

The other category of law within Judaism, that which pertains to the relation between the human being and God, *bayn Adam laMakom*, may be referred to as transcending legislation. In the social realm the construct is designed to thrust the human being into the core, and away from the border. In the transcending regulations, the commandments function relative to the human being's dialogue with God, with the intent of propelling the individual into the dimension of transcendence.

The importance of the individual's contribution to the fulfillment of God's will is driven home quite forcibly in the castigation of Isaiah that the people's fear of God is "a commandment of men learned by rote" (Isaiah, 29:13). An instructive commentary to this terminology, "learned by rote," is that one who does only what one is commanded and does not add of one's own, does not do so out of a desire or will to (RaDak, ad. loc., in Mikraot Gedolot, 1951).

Thus, the law is the jumping off point, and the real spirit of the law is captured in adding the human ingredient to it. The programmed individual who is perfunctorily exact, but has reduced the self to a lifeless person not responding to situations in the freedom and spontaneity of human conscience within Judaic guidelines, is roundly condemned.

The concept of self is very much in demand for the proper actualization of God's will to unfold. In allowing Scripture and the Talmud to speak for themselves, it appears perfectly obvious that it is not *in* the law, but rather, in social legislation, *within* the law, and, in transcending legislation, *through* the law, that authentic Judaism is expressed. The law is thus the carefully constructed framework which is intended to elicit the highest level of one's social and spiritual self.

References

Appel, G.)Ed.) (1970). *Samuel K. Mirsky memorial volume: Studies in Jewish law, philosophy, and literature.* New York: Yeshiva University Press.
Branden, N. (1974). *The Disowned self.* New York: Bantam Books.
Frankl, V.E. (1963). *Man's search for meaning: An introduction to logotherapy.* New York: Washington Square Press.
The Holy Scriptures (3 vols.) (1982). Philadelphia: Jewish Publication Society.
Jerusalem Talmud (5 vols.) (1968). New York: Otzar Haseforim.
Karo, J. (16th cent.). *Shulhan Arukh* (10 vols.) (1965). New York: M.P. Press.
Maimonides, M. (12th cent.). *Mishnah Torah* (6 vols.) (1962). New York; M.P. Press.
Maslow, A.H. (1970). *Motivation and personality.* New York: Harper and Row.
Maslow, A.H. (1971). *Religions, values, and peak-experiences.* New York: Viking Press.
The Midrash (10 vols.) (1961). H. Freedman & M. Simon (Eds.). London: Soncino Press.
Mikraot Gedolot (10 vols.) (1951). New York: Pardes.
Rosenzweig, F. (1955). *On Jewish learning.* New York: Schocken Books.

The Talmud (18 vols.) (1961). I. Epstein (Ed.). London: Soncino Press.
Vitz, P.C. (1983). *Psychology as religion: The cult of self-worship.* Grand Rapids, Michigan: Eardmans Publishing Co.
Weiss, R.S. (1975). *Marital separation.* New York: Basic Books.
Yankelovich, D. (1982). *New rules: Searching for self-fulfillment in a world turned upside down.* New York: Bantam Books.

Psycho-*Halakhic* Man of Conscience*

LEVI MEIER, Ph.D., is Chaplain of Cedars-Sinai Medical Center and psychotherapist in private practice in Los Angeles, CA. He also serves as Adjunct Professor at Yeshiva University of Los Angeles, lecturing on "Psychology and Judaism." He received his M.S. in Gerontology and Ph.D. in Psychology from the University of Southern California. Rabbi Meier was ordained at Yeshiva University where he received an M.A. in Jewish Philosophy. He draws upon his varied and extensive clinical and educational background as he serves interchangeably as rabbi, psychotherapist, gerontologist and thanatologist. His book "Jewish Values in Bioethics," published by Human Sciences Press, appeared in the summer (1986).

ABSTRACT: After establishing the centrality of conscience, via the Jewish concepts of *Imitatio Dei* and *Lifnim Mishurat Hadin*, a psycho-*Halakhic* man of conscience is described. In contrast, *Halakhic* man is depicted as man-as-object to the exclusion of man-as-subject. In this paradigm of the *Halakhic* man, all human needs are known *a priori*. To allow for man-as-subject, the psycho-*Halakhic* man is created. The fusion of man-as-object and man-as-subject is accomplished via man's conscience. Conscience struggles to understand the essence of Judaism and equilibrates the object/subject dichotomy. The psycho-*Halakhic* man of conscience is in a constant dynamic balance.

I-Conscience

In the fall of 1985, I offered a course at the Jewish Studies Institute of Yeshiva University of Los Angeles entitled "Conscience and Autonomy within Jewish Tradition." Although the course contained readings from such seminal modern Orthodox Jewish philosophers and theologians as Rabbi Joseph Soloveitchik, Rabbi Samuel Belkin, Rabbi Aharon Lichtenstein, Rabbi Eliezer Berkovits, and Rabbi David Hartman, what ultimately proved most significant were the comments of students and colleagues who chose *not* to enroll in the course.

Their remarks reflected two stimulating and provocative areas of thought. One was that the subject matter to be taught constituted an area that it was best not to explore in serious and systematic fashion; that it was a "road less traveled" (Peck, 1979), posing the same risks as an investigation into *Pardes*. *Pardes* literally means "paradise" and figuratively refers to philosophy and mysticism. The *Talmud* (*Hagigah*, 14b) relates the story of four great Rabbis, Rabbis Akiba, Ben

---

*Man is used to mean mankind and includes woman as well.

Zoma, Ben Azzai, and Aher, who engaged in esoteric studies in the second century c.e. These four were said to have "entered paradise." Ben Azzai studied mysticism and died, Ben Zoma "saw" and lost his reason, and Aher became an apostate. Only Rabbi Akiba entered in peace and came out in peace (Scholem, 1965, p. 57). My would-be students apparently felt that a study of "Conscience and Autonomy within Jewish Tradition" was potentially too intimidating a task to undertake, bearing too much similarity to an inquiry into *Pardes* (Linzer, 1984, chapter 1).

The other reason behind the students' reluctance to enroll in my course was that they were convinced *a priori* that anyone who genuinely explored the issue of conscience could not maintain his traditional Jewish practices and beliefs. They believed that Judaism does not allow for one's individual conscience to be expressed.

This introductory investigation hopes to demonstrate not only that conscience *is* discussed within the Jewish tradition, but that it forms an essential aspect of Jewish thought. The centrality of conscience is most poignantly expressed by R. Aryeh Leib Heller in the introduction to his *Kezot ha-Hoshen*, an eighteenth century study on civil, economic, and legal jurisprudence as outlined in the Code of Jewish Law (*Karo, Shulhan Arukh, Hoshen Mishpat*): "The *Torah* was not given to angels (*Talmud, Berakhot*, 25b), but to human beings who have been endowed with human faculties and abilities."

Rabbi Heller emphasized the paradoxical aspect of Judaism. Judaism, a *divinely* revealed religion, can only be comprehended via *human* understanding. This paradox of the interrelatedness of Divinity–humanity constitutes the core issue underlying conscience.

What is conscience? And what is the relationship of conscience to a revealed religion?

The unabridged edition of the *Random House Dictionary of the English Language* defines conscience as "the sense of what is right or wrong in one's conduct or motives, impelling one toward right action" (Stein, 1967). No Jewish encyclopedia has an entry on "conscience." Conscience is covered in most standard encyclopedias, with the *Encyclopedia of Religion and Ethics* (1952) devoting part of its general article on conscience to the place of this concept within Judaism. The article, however, is a general exposition of Jewish ethics, as if ethics and conscience were identical.

Is a sense of what is right or wrong derived from a Divinely revealed *Torah*, or from an autonomous self? Assuming that a sense of right and wrong is derived from the *Torah*, what was the source of right and wrong prior to revelation?

The *Midrash* comments that Noah, Abraham, Isaac, and Jacob observed the commandments of the *Torah* (*Midrash Rabbah*, Genesis 26:5;32:5). Whether this *Midrash* is to be understood literally or figuratively is a moot point (Heineman, 1954), p. 106). However, it is clear that most people who lived prior to the revelation were not endowed with sufficient intuitive ability to observe by their own initiative the ethical commandments of the *Torah* as were Noah, Abraham, Isaac, and Jacob. How, then, did other people develop a sense of what was right? The *Talmud* states:

> "Rabbi Yohanan observed: If the *Torah* had not been given, we could have learned modesty from the cat, honesty from the ant, chastity from the dove, and good manners from the cock" (*Talmud, Erubin*, 100b).

This significant passage implies that a sense of right and wrong not only predates revelation, but that it is an inherent part of a more universal revelation—that of the creation of the world. Through nature, man can learn virtuous behavior.

The Rabbis of the *Mishnah* recognized that natural morality has always existed. The *Mishnah* states: "Rabbi Elazar ben Azariah says: If there is no *Torah* there is no *derekh eretz* (natural morality) and without natural morality there is no *Torah*" (*Mishnah, Abot*, 3:17). The Hebrew expression *derekh eretz* literally means "the way of the land," and refers to all the things which are necessary for the sustenance of life. Therefore, *derekh eretz* at times could refer to professionalism or sexual relations or general worldliness or social mores or ethics and morality. Rabbi Samson Raphael Hirsch defines *derekh eretz* as encompassing:

> ... the situations arising from and dependent upon the circumstance that the earth is the place where the individual must live, fulfill his destiny and dwell together with others and that he must utilize resources and conditions provided on earth in order to live and to accomplish his purpose. Accordingly, the term *derekh eretz* is used primarily to refer to ways of earning a living, to the social order that prevails on earth, as well as to the mores and considerations of courtesy and propriety arising from social living and also to things pertinent to good breeding and general education (Hirsch, 1978, p. 434).

In this context, Rabbenu Yonah interprets *derekh eretz* as referring to ethical virtues and morality (*Mishnah, Abot*, 3:17).

Natural morality and Torah complement one another. Although both co-exist and enhance one another in guiding mankind toward ethical behavior, each domain exists independently of the other as well.

The *Midrash* states: "Rabbi Yishmael, the son of Rabbi Nachman said: for twenty-six generations, *derekh eretz* (natural morality) preceded the

Torah" (Midrash Rabbah, Leviticus, 9:3). The twenty-six generations refer to the span of time from the creation of the world until the giving of the *Torah*. This statement implies that natural morality not only existed prior to revelation, but also forms the basis of the *Torah*.

In reflecting on man's search for what is right or wrong, it is axiomatic that man prior to revelation and man post-revelation have had the same opportunity to live an ethical life. It is logically and philosophically untenable to assume that God could create a potentially more meaningful life or a potentially more ethical way of living for one period in human history than for a prior epoch in that history.

If man's conscience assisted him in his search for good, why was revelation necessary at all? Furthermore, has the function of conscience been superseded by Divine revelation? What is the role of conscience in the post-revelation period? Does conscience conflict with Jewish Law or complement it?

My thesis is that conscience complements Jewish Law. A manifestation of the complementary nature of conscience to Jewish thought and law is the concept of *Lifnim Mishurat Hadin*, a mode of behavior that goes "beyond the letter of the law." The *Torah* anticipates that there will arise occasions upon which mankind will be required to pursue higher moral standards and guide itself by an even nobler mode of conduct than that which is prescribed in the *Torah* itself (Spero, 1983, p. 167; Shilo, 1978; Berman, 1977, 1975).

Nahmanides comments on "and you shall do what is right and good in the eyes of God:"

> Our Rabbis have a beautiful *Midrash* on this verse. They have said: ["that which is right and good"] refers to a compromise, and going beyond the requirement of the letter of the law. The intent of this is as follows: At first he [Moses] stated that you are to keep His [God's] statutes and His testimonies which He commanded you; and now He is formulating that even where, He has not commanded you, you must give thought as well to do what is good and right in His eyes, for He loves the good and the right.
>
> Now this is a great principle, for it is impossible to mention in the *Torah* all aspects of man's conduct with his neighbors and friends, and all his various transactions, and the ordinances of all societies and countries. But since He mentioned many of them—such as, *Thou shalt not go up and down as a talebearer, Thou shalt not take vengeance, nor bear any grudge; neither shalt Thou stand idly by the blood of Thy neighbor; Thou shalt not curse the deaf; Thou shalt rise up before the hoary head,* and the like—He reverted to state in a general way that in all matters, one should do what is good and right, including even compromise and going beyond the requirements of the law.
>
> Other examples are the Rabbis' ordinances concerning the prerogative of a neighbor, and even what they said [concerning the desirability] that

one's youthful reputation be unblemished, and that one's conversation with people be pleasant. Thus [a person must seek to refine his behavior] in every form of activity, until he is worthy of being called "good and upright" (Nahmanides, Deuteronomy, 6:18).

Nahmanides reiterates this notion in his comments on *you shall be holy*:

> Therefore, after having listed the matters which He prohibited altogether, Scripture followed them by a general command that we practice moderation even in matters which are permitted ... Similarly, he [man] should keep himself away from impurity [in his ordinary daily activity], even though we have not been admonished against it in the *Torah* ... And such is the way of the *Torah*, that after it lists certain specific prohibitions, it includes them all in a general precept.
>
> Thus, after warning with detailed laws regarding all business dealings between people, such as not to steal or rob or to wrong one another, and other similar prohibitions, He said in general: 'And Thou shalt do that which is right and good', thus including under a positive commandment the duty of doing that which is right, and of agreeing to a compromise [when not to do so would be inequitable]; as well as all requirements to act beyond the line of justice [i.e., to be generous in not insisting upon one's rights as defined by the strict letter of the law, but to agree to act beyond that line of the strict law].
>
> The *Torah* has admonished us against immorality and forbidden foods, but has permitted sexual intercourse between man and wife, and the eating of [certain] meat and wine. If so, a man of desire could consider this to be a permission to be passionately addicted to sexual intercourse with his wife or many wives, and be among wine bibbers, among gluttonous eaters of flesh, and speak freely all profanities, since this prohibition has not been [expressly] mentioned in the *Torah*, and thus he will become a sordid person within the permissible realm of the *Torah* (Nahmanides, Leviticus, 19:2)

Both passages accentuate the fact that conducting oneself ethically requires much more than what is prescribed specifically in the *Torah*. Most significant, however, is that the emphasis upon transcending the normative guidelines is indeed an integral part of the *Torah* and Jewish law. Conscience does not consist of a metalegal dimension but a specific legal structure.

Lifnim Mishurat Hadin has been operationalized in various ways in *Talmudic* literature. Following the letter of the law exclusively was ascribed as a factor leading to the destruction of Jerusalem. The *Talmud* states:

> "That they shall do"—this means [acts] within the requirements of the law. For Rabbi Johanan said: Jerusalem was destroyed only because they

gave judgments therein in accordance with Biblical law. Were they then to have judged in accordance with untrained arbitrators? But say thus: because they based their judgments [strictly] upon Biblical law, and did not go within the requirements of the law" (*Talmud, Baba Mezia*, 30b).

The national calamity of the destruction of Jerusalem and the Temple was ascribed not to a lack of proper observances, but to several reasons including, mankind's acting only according to the letter of the law and not observing "*beyond* the letter of the law." Thus, unless conscience is acted upon, the whole *raison d'etre* of observant Jewish life is rendered significantly deficient. Although the *Torah* does not and cannot prescribe the proper dictates of the heart in all potential circumstances, the philosophy of purpose of the *Torah* is to create a human being who constantly seeks to uncover a higher moral or spiritual purpose (Belkin, 1978, pp. 14–19).

This is indeed the meaning of the word "*Torah*." The Greeks (Septuagint) translated *Torah* as *Nomos* (law), "probably in the sense of a living network of traditions and customs of a people. The designation of the *Torah* by *Nomos* and by its Latin successor *lex*, has historically given rise to the sad misunderstanding that *Torah* means legalism" (*Encyclopaedia Judaica*, 1971, 15:1238–1239).

Thus, Judaism was misapprehended to be primarily a religion of law. Fulfillment of proper ritual was misperceived as constituting sufficient adherence to Judaism. *Torah* in fact comes from the Hebrew root word which means "teaching." Teaching embodies "law and philosophy, *Talmud* and Bible, manifestation and essence" (Leeuw, 1938). It also encompasses norms and spirituality, theology and historical experiences, and finally the letter of the law and the spirit of the law (conscience). The teaching of *Torah* must create a Jewish religious consciousness that integrates a normative legal system *with* spirituality, creating not a *Halakhic* man (Soloveitchik, 1983), but rather a *Halakhic* man of conscience. Although *Halakhah* includes conscience, it nevertheless has to be accentuated as the *Halakhic* man of conscience.

Etymologically, the word conscience means "with knowledge." The core of conscience allows one to have a panoramic view of all knowledge, a sense of interrelatedness of knowledge, facts and emotions. This totality creates a gestalt, whereby physical, biological and psychological phenomena form a new unit.

The *Halakhic* man of conscience concerns himself with the process of becoming intuitively righteous. The purpose of *Halakhah* (Jewish law) is to serve as a means of achieving the highest human potential: *Imitatio Dei*, emulating God's Divine attributes or actions, including justice and mercy. This religious philosophy of purpose affords a *raison d'etre* to man's continued existence. The purpose of man's existence is to sanctify God by emulating Him, which makes man an associate of God.

Another operational definition of *Lifnim Mishurat Hadin* is exhibited in a celebrated *Talmudic* passage, in which following the strict law is subordinated to following the spirit of the law:

> Some porters [negligently] broke a barrel of wine belonging to Rabbah bar Hanah. Thereupon he seized their garments: So they went and complained to Rab. "Return their garments to them," he ordered. "Is that the law?," he enquired. "Yes," he rejoined: "'That Thou mayest walk in the way of good men'." Their garments having been returned, they observed, "We are poor men, have worked all day, and are in need; are we to get nothing?" "Go and pay them," he ordered. "Is that the law?" he enquired "Yes," was his reply, " 'And keep the path of the righteous' " (*Talmud, Baba Mezia*, 83a).

Although the workers were negligent, Rab told Rabbah bar Hanah that in such a case one should not insist on the letter of the law (i.e., withhold the workers' pay). Living "beyond the letter of the law" required in this instance not only a transition to a higher standard of morality, it demanded direct *opposition* to the letter of the law. This episode demonstrated that acting according to one's conscience is not merely a step toward a higher level of moral conduct within the same continuum, but represents a quantum leap to a qualitatively different plane. Here the law yielded to something beyond itself—something that could not be codified, but only perceived in the unique situation that presented itself. The moral agent had to make a judgment, taking into account not only the law but also an inner voice which could not be suppressed.

Conscience focuses not on what is, but on what ought to be. Thus, conscience is essentially intuitive. Conscience manifests itself by demonstrating the interrelatedness of the totality of man's knowledge. It is the task of conscience to reveal the one course of action that is required; the unique possibility to be selected by a specific person in a specific situation. Only conscience is capable of adjusting and applying the eternal law to the specific situation. Only conscience is capable of adjusting and applying the eternal law to the specific situation in which a flesh-and-blood individual finds himself. Living one's conscience means living perpetually on a highly personalized level, aware of the full moral concreteness of each situation.

Having determined the central role of conscience and how it has been operationalized in *Talmudic* literature, how can one be certain that one is functioning with a pure conscience in the various situations and circumstances which confront man, rather than with an "ordinary" conscience which is not based on *Torah* values?

Purity of conscience may well be an impossible achievement. Man is born into a certain family, a particular culture and *milieu*, a specific time in history, and with very specific genetic endowments. The dictates of one's heart are inevitably influenced by all these factors and more. Family values, the special influences of the cohort generation and the limitations of the biopsychosocial conditions all play a role in the formation of conscience.

This awareness of the uniqueness of each individual human being is fundamental in understanding the special nature of every human being's conscience. The *Midrash* states: "Just as the physical features of everyone differ from one another, so do their values" (*Midrash Rabbah*, Numbers, 21). Thus, both the physical make-up and value system of every person are different from those of every other human being.

Unlike Nahmanides, Maimonides understands the concept of *Lifnim Mishurat Hadin* as referring to conduct which is only applicable to an elitist, pious sect. Maimonides states: "And the early pietists would incline their traits from the median path toward either extreme. One trait they would incline toward the one extreme, another toward the other extreme, and this is *Lifnim Mishurat Hadin*" (*Mishnah Torah, Deut*, 1:5).

Maimonides, however, subsumes character development and ethical sensitivity under the demand of *Imitatio Dei* (Deuteronomy, 28:9). He states: "And we are commanded to walk in these median paths and they are the right and the good paths, as it is written, 'And you shall walk in His ways' " (*Mishnah Torah, Deot*, 1:5). This passage refers to a sense of striving for an ideal, rather than of satisfying basic demands. The ethic of *Imitatio Dei* is not just a lofty ideal reserved for an elite, aristocratic, pious few, but a pressing obligation.

Thus, both Nahmanides and Maimonides concur on the significance of pursuing a higher universal ethic than that which is prescribed in the *Torah*, but differ in pinpointing the *Halakhic* rubric from which it springs. Nahmanides views conscience as part of the *Halakhic* system of *Lifnim Mishurat Hadin*, while Maimonides views conscience as part of the commandment of *Imitatio Dei*. Thus, the pursuit of a higher moral obligation is part and parcel of the *Halakhic* system; it is not optional, but becomes as compulsory as the legal requirements themselves. The complementary nature of conscience to law is part of the *Halakhic* system. The legal texts themselves introduce moral considerations into the legal process. The *Halakhah* also saw that the "higher law" was ordained by the law itself (Landman, 1969, pp. 18–20).

Despite the fact that law and conscience are both rooted in the Divine

Halakhic system, the methods employed in arriving at a specific action within each realm proceeds according to vastly different lines of reasoning.

"Law" refers to a set of statutes which regulate an individual's overall conduct by means of established behavioral guidelines. It also refers to one's expressed words, thoughts, and feelings. In contrast, "conscience" calls for thoughtful, deliberate action in a specific case under very special circumstances. In the realm of conscience, every case is phenomenologically different. The differences are so crucial that no meaningful directives can be formulated; every decision is a personal one. The "higher law" varies from individual to individual (Landman, 1969, p. 19).

In the area of conscience, the *Halakhic* norm becomes situational. Whether the overall guideline is *Imitatio Dei* or *Lifnim Mishurat Hadin*, it suggests a general direction and not a series of specifically prescribed acts. Conscience depends on circumstances and may vary with the individual. Since no two individuals look alike or think alike, their conscience may guide them differently depending on how each perceives reality.

Reality exists only as it is perceived by the observer. The observer is conditioned by his unique and varied background. Although the *Torah*'s rules are absolute, Rabbinic legislation has provided latitude and flexibility by allowing those who observe Jewish law to perceive reality individually and act accordingly, based on their own conscience. This fluidity of *Halakhah* within the domains of *Imitatio Dei* or *Lifnim Mishurat Hadin* is also demonstrated by the Rabbinic concept of "this is the law, but it is not to be publicized" (*Talmud, Shabbat* 12b). A *Halakhic* man of conscience can allow himself flexibility and leniency under specific circumstances; such decisions, however, cannot be prescribed for others.

Another example of the fluidity available to the *Halakhic* man of conscience is the expression, "it is different in this case," a term found in *Talmudic* literature thousands of times (e.g., *Talmud, Baba Mezia*, 24a). This expression implies that even though a general rule of conduct may have been provided for certain situations, any slightly different variable within those situations—e.g. an elderly person rather than of an adult, a sick person rather than a healthy one, a drought rather than the normal amount of rain—is sufficient reason for the *Talmud* to say, "It is different here." In order words, while the rule still applies in general, it does not apply in this particular case.

For example, on *Yom Kippur* (The Day of Atonement) a Jew must abstain from five forms of activity, including washing himself. Other than the minimal cleaning of hands and eyes, washing and bathing is prohibited. One of the categories of people exempted from this rule is a bride during her first thirty days after marriage. The importance of connubial bliss at the beginning of a new marriage permitted this (washing) leniency (*Talmud, Yoma,* 73b), an exception clearly motivated by the communal *Halakhic* man of conscience.

The enhancement of human dignity, the quest for domestic peace, and the mitigation or alleviation of anxiety or pain is an integral part of the *Halakhic*-conscience process. These factors have not only evolved into *Halakhic* norms themselves, but have done so due to the necessity of *Halakhic*-conscience (Lichtenstein, 1975, p. 67).

Although Marvin Fox (1979) allows for the possibility of an ethic which is independent of the *Halakhah*, he does not accept the textual proofs of *Lifnim Mishurat Hadin* nor the *Talmudic* passage indicating that it would have been possible to imitate certain forms of animal behavior for the maintenance of an ordered society and to achieve good personal relations (*Talmud, Erubin*, 100b; Urbach, 1969, pp. 286–287).

His objection to *Lifnim Mishurat Hadin* reiterates the fact that the requirement to be holy (Leviticus, 19:2) is presented in the *Torah* as a Divine mandate. Furthermore, Nahmanides speaks explicitly of the fact that this verse is a commandment (Fox, 1979, pp. 14–15). Fox's objection is valid regarding the title of Aharon Lichtenstein's (1975) essay, "Does Jewish Tradition Recognize an Ethic *Independent* of the Halakha?," yet it only serves to further validate that the impetus to transcend *Halakhah* is an indigenous aspect of the *Halakhic* system. "Independence of the *Halakhah*," is not the central consideration; the Divine mandate creating the *Halakhic*-conscience is compelling. Thus, the *Torah* recommends or even prescribes proper action even when such action may transcend and differ from the requirements of the law.

In reference to "If the *Torah* had not been given, we could have learned modesty from the cat . . ." (*Talmud, Erubin*, 100b), Fox maintains "that this would not bring us to a knowledge of our *duty* to behave in this way" (Fox, 1979, p. 13). He maintains that both law and independent morality require some ground of obligation. If independent morality is based on a prudential decision then there is no awareness of being duty bound.

However, both Saadya Gaon and Maimonides maintain that mankind would have been able to evolve a code of moral laws based on man's innate pursuit of ethical and saintly behavior. Maimonides states explicitly that someone who has no desire for shedding of blood, theft, robbery, fraud—things which all people commonly agree are evils—are to be more praised than he who desires these evils but restrains his passions (Twersky, 1972, p. 378; Altmann, 1969, pp. 94–105).

Thus, the contrary of Fox's contention is accurate. Independent morality meritoriously supersedes Divinely commanded ethical behavior.

II – Psycho-*Halakhic* Man

At the beginning of this essay, I referred to the essential paradox of Judaism: that although the *Torah* was given by God, the words of the *Torah* can only be understood by human beings. It has been demonstrated that the Divinity-humanity fusion creates a *Halakhic* man of conscience.

Not only under special circumstances, but also in fundamental basics, the *Halakhic* man of conscience is involved in various interpretations of the *Torah*. The *Torah* directs us to honor and give reverence to our father and mother (Exodus, 20:12 and Leviticus, 19:3). The *Talmud* defines honor as positive acts of personal service, including feeding and dressing one's parent. Reverence is defined as the avoidance of disrespectful acts; rabbinic examples include not sitting in a parent's seat or speaking before parents, and never contradicting them (*Talmud, Kiddushin*, 31b).

Is the definition of a parent strictly a biological one, (*Talmud, Yevamot*, 22a and b) with no significance attached to the parenting skills one may or may not possess? Is a parent still a parent if he/she is engaged in child molestation or child abuse? What is the status of "parents" who have adopted newborn babies?

Although the Responsa literature deals with many of these questions, ultimately even the "clear" law of honoring and revering one's parents is frequently left to the realm of the *Halakhic* man of conscience (Blidstein, 1975). Adults who were victimized as children by their parents, for example, must necessarily differ in their response in honoring and revering their parents. Also, one's individual pain threshold plays a role. Some children, upon reaching middle-aged adulthood, may be capable of understanding that their parents were mentally ill, while others may have been hurt so badly that they are unable to perceive their parents as merely ill rather than evil.

Psychological predisposition also plays a role in the creation of the *Halahkic* man of conscience. Every person has an individualized psyche. This is most clearly demonstrated by giving a mental status examination to both patients and non-patients. Every person achieves a *singular* score in thought patterns, perceptions and affect.

Allow me, therefore, to suggest a new category of psycho-*Halakhic* man: the psycho-*Halakhic* man of conscience. While neither exclusively a psychological man nor a man of conscience, he has elements of both. He is also not exclusively a *Halakhic* man, although *Halakhah* is a primary element in his life.

Man experiences the world as a subject, as an object, and at times as a fusion of subject and object. These three different experiences of reality reflect different responses on the part of the psycho-*Halakhic* man of conscience.

Man-as-subject experiences the world as different from himself. The world is not the man, but at the same time the world makes sense only as it bears some relationship to man as the subject who perceives it.

Man, the subject, is located in physical space and time, and possesses desires, feelings, and fears. Man-as-subject sees objects from a point of view. He experiences life from a point of view that is limited, but it is exactly that limitation that provides a boundary offering stability and definition to experience.

As man-as-subject experiences the world each day, his experience forms a continuity with what he underwent yesterday, last year, and thirty years ago. All of this represents a point of orientation, in terms of which man-as-subject organizes and gives meaning to his experience.

A second aspect of man-as-subject involves the exercise of power in relation to the world around man. This power affords man some control over what he experiences. Man can translate his desires into changes in the world and observe the effect of his action.

Man as subject has both an orienting point of reference and is also an active agent. Laing has stated the matter in the following way:

> I wish to define a person in a twofold way; in terms of experience, as a center of orientation of the objective universe; and in terms of behavior, as the origin of actions. Personal experience transforms a given field into a field of intention and action; only through action can our experience be transformed (Laing, 1967, p. 8).

A third aspect of man-as-subject is that of man as a party in a relationship. When someone relates to man-as-subject, man-as-subject fully understands that the other party is trying to effect a change in man-as-subject's organization of the world. Thus, man-as-subject is not only a body which communicates, but an ever evolving consciousness concerned with how he is giving meaning to the world.

Man-as-subject does not objectify. Attributes are not given to the self in this experience; man is the "observer," not the "observed." Man-as-object, however, does objectify and assign attributes. Man-as-object is the object of attention.

The experience of man-as-subject is immediate. This man only "lives."

In contrast, man-as-object is a man mediated by symbols, and he is "known" rather than "lived." Man-as-object is the experience of self-scrutinization and constant evaluation. This requires the ability to reflect upon oneself. Man-as-object is inevitable. However, when man-as-object becomes so pervasive in the experiential life of the individual that man-as-subject is eclipsed, pathology ensues.

Man-as-object has essential characteristics and experiences that define *what* he is. This stands in contrast to the notion of man-as-subject, which concerns itself with the more prosaic fact *that* man exists.

Man-as-subject talks in such terms as " 'I' think of an idea," " 'I' desire to play tennis," and " 'I' fear dying."

Subjectivity itself thus turns out to be not only an intentionality—a meaning conferring ability—but a relationship. It is impossible to have an objective relationship to anything at all; at the very least it would be intentional and thus subjective (Poole, 1972, p. 95). Kierkegaard stated:

> With reference to religion—subjectivity is truth. The objection to objectivity is a subjective one, coming as it does from a passionate involvement with the ethical responsibility of the thinking individual. Thinkerless thought is mere objectivity—it is a failure of responsibility.
>
> What is accepted as true is accepted as true because of an already existing structure of *belief* in the individual, an existing structure of interest or fear.
>
> The answer to Pilate's famous question is that there is no truth, only truths (Kierkegaard, 1941, p. 171).

Man-as-object reflects upon our desires, fears, and thoughts. We name them, judge them, reason with regard to them and have feelings about them. With dispassionate detachment, man-as-object reflects upon himself.

The "I" experience allows for becoming, while the "objectified me" may contain aspects of bad faith (Sartre, 1956, Part 1, Chapter 2).

The psycho-*Halakhic* man of conscience maintains an intricate balance of *subject* and *object*. Psychopathology is manifest when man functions only as subject or only as object.

William James also integrates the objective and subjective as comprising a part of the religious man. James states that to multitudes of peoples, objective truth represents an ideal refuge. Theology has never tolerated probable truths. The multitude aspire to a dogmatic theology which is arrived at in *a priori* manner. Yet, James concludes:

> The world of our experience consists at all times of two parts, an objective and a subjective part, of which the former may be incalculably more ex-

tensive than the latter, and yet the latter can never be omitted or suppressed. Religion is the unique combination of objective theocentric theological truths and the subjective phenomena regarding these truths which are expressed in terms of an anthropocentive view of life (James, 1958, p. 377–378).

Furthermore, surveying the field of comparative religion, it is noted that although a great variety of theological and philosophical thought prevails among mankind, the human feelings engendered by religious observance are almost always the same.

Thus, the objective theories generated by religions, are secondary; the essence of religion involves the more constant element and expression of feeling. James quotes Professor Leuba:

> God is not known, He is not understood; He is used—sometimes as meat-purveyor, sometimes as moral support, sometimes as friend, sometimes as an object of love. If He proves Himself useful, the religious consciousness asks for no more than that. Does God really exist? How does he exist? What is he? are so many irrelevant questions. Not God, but life, more life, a larger, richer, more satisfying life is in the last analysis, the end of religion. The love of life, at one and every level of development, is the religious impulse (James, 1958, p. 382).

The theocentric view of religion is significant to the degree that it has an impact on anthropocentrism.

Julius Guttmann, the distinguished scholar of Jewish philosophy, also expresses his own view on the relationship between objective Divine law and subjective man. He states that the commandments are the conduit for living a holy life. This behavior allows for religious expression of feelings as well. Furthermore, the commandments must themselves be liberated from their strictly ritualistic context and re-adapted to their original context of religious intended behavior. At times the legalism of the law creates the artificial appearance of "religious" life (Guttmann, 1955, pp. 274–275).

Guttmann provides an example which demonstrates the subject-object dichotomy as well. Naturally, he reminds us, there is a Divine command to pray to God. However, if by chance one has forgotten to include the special "New Moon" paragraph, one is obligated to repeat one's prayer in its entirety. Guttmann maintains that such stringent requirements literally eliminate religious expression within Judaism for the sake of maintaining the legal system. The underlying thesis of Guttmann's philosophy is that *man* must not be eliminated from the objective law.

Interestingly, Rabbinic codifiers have alluded to this concept as well. The Rabbis were asked to respond to an inquiry regarding whether a person who prays without proper religious devotion is obliged to repeat his prayers. In conceptual terminology, it would be phrased as, "Can a person fulfill his obligation to pray as a man-object (an 'I - It' relationship) without having been in the state of a man-subject (an 'I-Thou' relationship)?" The Rabbis responded that since it is nearly impossible to thrust man into an I-Thou relationship on demand, he is not obligated to repeat his prayers (Karo, *Shulhan Arukh, Orah Hayyim*, 101:1). Two case vignettes will concretize our theory:

> The beloved daughter of Rabbi Elijah Pruzna (Feinstein) took sick about a month before she was to be married and after a few days was rapidly sinking. Rabbi Elijah's son entered into the room where R. Elijah, wrapped in *tallit* and *tefillin*, was praying with the congregation, to tell him that his daughter was in her death throes. R. Elijah went into his daughter's room and asked the doctor how much longer it would be until the end. When he received the doctor's reply, Rabbi Elijah returned to his room, removed his Rashi's *tefillin*, and quickly put on the *tefillin* prescribed by *Rabbenu Tam*, for immediately upon his daughter's death, he would be an *onen*, a mourner whose dead relative has not as yet been buried, and as such would be subject to the law that an *onen* is exempt from all commandments. After he removed his second pair of *tefillin*, wrapped them up, and put them away, he entered his dying daughter's room, in order to be present at the moment his most beloved daughter of all would return her soul back to its Maker. We have here great strength and presence of mind, the acceptance of the Divine decree with love, the consciousness of the law and the judgment, the might and power of the *Halakhah*, and faith, strong like flint (Soloveitchik, 1983, pp. 77–78).

This is an example of Rabbi Soloveitchik's view of the *Halakhic* man. Does this *Halakhic* man allow himself to be a psycho-Halakhic man of conscience? How would the psycho-*Halakhic* man of conscience have reacted?

Event	Hypothesis: Man as *Subject-Object* psycho-*Halakhic* man of conscience	Hypothesis: Man as *Object* *Halakhic* man
1) Rabbi Elijah's most beloved daughter is about to be married.	1) Rabbi Elijah *feels* elated about the forthcoming marriage.	1) Rabbi Elijah *reflects* about his daughter's marriage and the meaning this has for her and her husband, as well as any implication this meaning has for him.

Event	Hypothesis: Man as *Subject-Object* psycho-*Halakhic* man of conscience	Hypothesis: Man as *Object* *Halakhic* man
2) A month before the forthcoming marriage, Rabbi Elijah's daughter becomes ill.	2) Rabbi Elijah *feels* sad and hopes for his daughter's speedy recovery.	2) Rabbi Elijah *reflects* on the meaning of the juxtaposition of his daughter's illness and the forthcoming marriage.
3) Her condition deteriorates rapidly.	3) Rabbi Elijah *feels* anger toward God.	3) Rabbi Elijah mentally disengages from his daughter's critical illness and continues his normal activity of praying with his congregation.
4) Rabbi Elijah's prayers are interrupted and he is informed that his daughter is in her death throes. Rabbi Elijah asks the doctor how much longer his daughter will live.	4) Rabbi Elijah is perplexed, confused, and cries out for help from God and asks for support from his family and friends.	4) Rabbi Elijah sees only his *Halakhic* reality of desiring to fulfill the will of God by putting on another pair of *tefillin* before that opportunity is denied to him by his daughter's death.
5) Rabbi Elijah puts on another pair of *tefillin* and then returns to his daughter's room, at which time she dies.	5) Rabbi Elijah engages God in the issues of "Job" and feels totally isolated.	5) Rabbi Elijah ascribes meaning to his daughter's death, which is reflected by his quickly putting on *tefillin* prior to her death.

Although there may be some mutuality and overlap in events one, two, three, and four, event five diametrically distinguishes the two hypotheses. The *Halakhic* man acts as man-as-object; while the psycho-*Halakhic* man of conscience fuses the subject-object dichotomy. Rabbi Soloveitchik's view of *Halakhic* man is primarily that of man-as-object: *Halakhic* reality imposed on man's experiential reality. Man gives meaning to life's vicissitudes by submitting to the Divine *Halakhic* imperative.

This Divine imperative has no relationship to man's desires. Rabbi Simeon ben Gamaliel points out:

One should not say, "I do not want to eat meat together with milk; I do not want to wear clothes made of a mixture of wool and linen; I do not want to enter into an incestuous marriage," but he should say, "I do indeed want to, yet I must not, for my Father in Heaven has forbidden it (*Sifra*, Leviticus, 20:26).

Man-as-subject can also be a *Halakhic* man. Man-as-subject is not antithetical to *Halakhic* man. Man-as-subject contains the elements of the psycho-*Halakhic* man of conscience. This psycho-*Halakhic* man of conscience manifests the quintessential aspect of *Imitatio Dei* or *Lifnim Mishurat Hadin*.

Another case vignette is taken from my pastoral work as Chaplain at Cedars-Sinai Medical Center. A middle-aged woman related that as a child she had been physically and emotionally abused. As a young adult, she had decided to disengage from her mother because the abuse was still continuing, although in more subtle fashion.

The mother was now ill and had requested to see her daughter. The daughter, an observant Jewess, presented the issue of whether, according to Jewish law, she was now obligated to visit her mother.

How would *Halakhic* woman respond? And how would psycho-*Halakhic* woman respond? *Halakhic* woman would be guided above all by Jewish law; whatever decision is reached is not as relevant, in this context, as *how* this decision was arrived at. *Halakhic* woman looks at absolute facts, such as:

1) a mother,
2) a daughter,
3) the existence of child abuse,
4) an emotionally ill mother,
5) a mother's request, and
6) a middle-aged child having become disengaged from her mother.

The *Halakhic* woman fulfills the commandments of honoring one's mother and visits her mother.

Employing these criteria, the two women are perceived exclusively as objects. However, can subjectivity play a role in this *Halakhic* process? Can we focus on the mother and daughter not only as objects, but as subjects? Why is the mother requesting to see her daughter *now*? Can the mother talk to her daughter and say words to the effect that, "I'm sorry for what I did to you as a child?" Can the daughter share her dilemma with her mother? Can all these real experiences take place to bring about not a *Halakhic*-woman but a psycho-*Halakhic* woman of conscience (Blidstein, 1975, pp. 130–136)?

III – Psycho-*Halakhic* Man of Conscience

Judaism is based on obedience to God. Through conscience, it is not God who is being heard, but the inner voice of man. The Jew, however, is required to listen to God's word.

What is conscience?

Does it refer to an autonomous view, whereby man recognizes in conscience what is right and what is wrong? This recognition does not consist of hearing an external judgment – i.e., the will of God – but is an internal act of recognizing the moral truth. Conscience is an affirmation of our sense of right, very often in conflict with the judgment of society, with the religious structure and possibly even with God himself.

Thus, conscience is an affirmation of ethical humanism, of the moral self-sufficiency of man, who in the final analysis must make his own judgments. Professor Isaiah Leibowitz claims that conscience is an atheistic category in Judaic thought (Leibowitz, 1979, pp. 14–15). Leibowitz emphasizes the dichotomy between the Kantian autonomy of man and the Jewish teaching of heteronomy (Falk, 1981, p. 66).

If conscience is understood in this way, it is not easily reconcilable with an ethic that looks to the word of God as its criterion of what is right. The Divine word is the judge of man's moral sense.

Conscience, however, can also be understood as the voice of God speaking to man in solitude. Man is able to determine what is right in *God's* view, not in man's. Wyschogrod states: "In this heteronomous view of conscience, there is no fundamental difference between obedience to God when God directly addresses man and listening to the voice of conscience in which it is also the voice of God that is being heard" (Wyschogrod, 1981, p. 321).

However, differentiating between an autonomous conscience driven by ethical humanism, and an heteronomous conscience generated by listening to the inner voice of God addressing man, is really semantic meaninglessness. Both forms of conscience are the voice of another calling us to our responsibility, along with realization that the voice at the same time seems to be coming from within us. On this level, God (who demands) and man (of whom the demand is made) are a unified whole (Wyschogrod, 1981, p. 323).

Within this discussion, an ethics of conscience has the potential of drifting into a Godless proclamation of human independence. After all, cannot man rely on himself to discover the good – not only universally and abstractly, but also in the concreteness of the existential situation in which conscience makes itself heard in judging the right of specific instances? It must be remembered, however, that this autonomous direction of conscience exists solely in relation to the Divine word. Conscience points beyond itself to the good or right which is *sensed* by conscience but not *created* by it (Wyschogrod, 1981, pp. 323–325).

In Biblical theology, it is the Divine word that is at the center of attention. Must the believing Jew therefore sacrifice his conscience in obeying God? May man give up an ultimate individuality when he embraces the covenant, knowing that the covenant has a more national character than an individual one? Is conscience the "Isaac" in each one of us, which we must be prepared to be offered on the altar of Divine sacrifice?

What is the relationship of obedience to God and one's conscience? Is not the very act of obedience ultimately dependent on the dictate of one's innermost conscience? Thus, even the act of submission on the part of man is affirmed in the depth of one's conscience. This is indeed the essence of the doctrine of free will, which is so crucial in the development of the spiritual personality (Deuteronomy 30:15). A Jew who remains faithful to the covenant is acting out of conscience and not social conformity.

The covenantal Jew is *ipso facto* a man of conscience. What happens when conscience and law conflict? If conscience is the motivating force behind the covenantal Jew, it must also be followed when conscience and law contradict one another. "If conscience is to have *any* authority, it must have all authority" (Wsychogrod, 1981, p. 327). Conscience must be obeyed even when it contradicts the Divine law as it is objectively understood. The law, as understood objectively, must be obeyed as one hears it *now* in the depth of one's conscience. Eugene Borowitz similarly understands Wsychogrod's (1981) contention

> that the individual conscience must be granted rights even when to us it appears to be acting in error. Not to do so would negate the very concept of conscience for a heteronomous revelation would have effectively usurped our God-given right to think and judge for ourselves (Borowitz, 1984, p. 50).

The well known *Talmudic* dictum: "For Rabbi Hanina said, He who is commanded and fulfills the command, is greater than he who fulfills it though not commanded (*Talmud, Kiddushin,* 31a)," seems to indicate a significant preference for an individual who obeys the commandment because it is commanded by God, rather than for someone who obeys commandments as a result of his conscience. However, Ephraim Urbach (1969) brilliantly interprets this comment contextually, as specifically referring to categories of people, such as non-Jews, women, and blind individuals which the *Torah* exempts from the performance of certain commandments or commandments in general (*Talmud, Baba Kamma,*

38a, 87a; Aodah Zarah, 3a). He specifically states that Rabbi Hanina was not emphasizing heteronomy over autonomy (Urbach, 1969, pp. 286–287).

The dialectic tension of autonomy and conscience within Judaism is succinctly expressed in the Hebrew word *Mitzvah*, which literally means commandment. However, with every *Mitzvah* there is a Divine law-giver, *Mitzave*, and a human law recipient, *Mitzuve*. The balance between all three of these elements highlights the significance of the role of conscience and autonomy within Judaism.

The opening line of the Code of Jewish law (Karo, *Shulhan Arukh, Orah Hayyim*) states: "A man should strengthen himself as a lion to get up in the morning to the service of his Creator." Rabbi Karo's beginning restates the outlook of Judah ben Tema, who suggested that a leonine resolve and other attributes are appropriate as one fulfills the will of God (*Mishnah, Abot*, 5:23). Rabbi Karo, however, wrote an introduction to the Code of Jewish law that was only printed once—in the Venice edition in 1565. In this introduction, he explains the purposes of the Code of Jewish law. Its first purpose is that a Rabbinic scholar should have the law easily accessible; and secondly, that the uninitiated students can easily find a guide to daily behavior. Thus, one can understand that the phrase calling upon man to "strengthen himself as a lion" to serve God was directed primarily toward uninitiated students, who desired to be guided exclusively by the *Halakhah*. However, for the person who is guided also by *Lifnim Mishurat Hadin* and *Imitatio Dei*, in contrast to the uninitiated student, the goal is also to internalize the *Halakhah* and follow one's conscience when deemed appropriate.

Rabbi Karo eliminated ideology and theology from the text of the *Shulhan Arukh*. It contains no philosophical prolegomenon. Rabbi Karo was not concerned with ethical underpinning or theological vision of *Halakhah*. The omission of these trans-*Halakhic* materials created a role of life characterized by regularity, routine, and stability. The absence of an ideational framework and a rationale of the law made it difficult for the Rabbinic scholar and the uninitiated student to utilize the *halakhic* concepts of *Lifnim Mishurat Hadin* and *Imitatio Dei* concomitantly with the practice of the law. "If the *Shulhan Arukh* only charts a specific way of life but does not impart a specific version or vision of meta-*Halakhah*, it is because the latter is to be supplied and experienced independently" (Twersky, 1982, pp. 142–143, 147, and footnote 43).

In order to listen to conscience, it is one's responsibility to have a conscience in good working order. There must be a willingness to listen to conscience—not only to what we want to hear, but to what conscience is actually saying, however painful its message may be. Furthermore, conscience needs to be sensitized and developed by God's revelation. God's revelation refers not only to the *Torah* but also to the more universal revelation of the history of mankind and the creation of the world (Maimonides, Basic Principles of the *Torah*, 2:1; Kings, 11:4 – uncensored version). Conscience does not necessarily mean acting autonomously. In order for conscience to be ethical it requires a well developed conscience. The development of an ethical conscience requires an elaborate process of education.

An autonomous conscience is differentiated from an heteronomous conscience. An autonomous conscience stems from one's inner voice. An heteronomous conscience is derived by a person's sense that one's inner voice is not a voice of solitude, but God addressing man.

The difficulty in ascertaining whether one's conscience is autonomous or heteronomous is that making such a determination is dependent on one's belief system; it is not a decision that can be verified empirically. It is not a situation in which the correspondence theory of truth is operational. This theory states that ideas and reality are in agreement with one another based on sense perception and our power of reason. The belief system that ultimately determines whether an autonomous or heteronomous conscience is functional is dependent on what is called a psychic truth.

Jung states a very basic and fundamental principle of psychology: physicality is not the only criterion of truth. There are also psychic truths. These psychic truths cannot be verified in any physical or empirical way.

Religious statements are in the category of psychic truths. They refer to things that cannot be established as physical facts. Psychic truths are independent of physical data. Religious statements are ultimately psychic confessions; such statements reflect our images of what is ineffable (Jung, 1973, pp. xi and xii). Similarly The Hymn of Glory expresses, "They imaged Thee, not as Thou art really; they described Thee by Thy acts only" (Birnbaum, 1949, p. 418).

Religious psychic truths have an objective and subjective side. The objective side is the *content* of religious belief; and the subjective side is the *form* in which this content is given to man, and the attitude that man adopts toward the content. The subjective side represents a personal faith, one which cannot be proved to someone who does not believe in it. This religious belief is not based on scientific proofs; it is an immediate certainty. This certainty in the object of faith is utterly personal (Guttmann, 1976, p. 23-25).

Conscience, whether autonomous or heteronomous, is a psychic phenomenon. And even when conscience contradicts one's objective understanding of the Divine law, the decision to follow the law or one's conscience is ultimately a manifestation of one's *psychic* understanding of God's revelation.

In contrast, Spero (1985) hypothesizes that there are two ways to acknowledge the religious patient's feelings and beliefs related to God. One way is to acknowledge these feelings as an aspect of the patient's psychological reality; a second approach accepts these feelings as actual phenomena. Spero's hypothesis has no practical significance in this context since all of man's actions ensue from psychological reality or actual phenomena. As Jung asserted, all religious statements are psychic truths and not amenable to verifiability.

IV-Implications for a Study of Psychology and Judaism

The study of psychology and Judaism is still in its infancy. Observations regarding the literature in psychology and Judaism have already been surveyed (Spero, 1980, 3-7). Dr. Reuven Bulka is to be credited for having started the *Journal of Psychology and Judaism* in 1976. This journal has provided a forum for a serious investigation of the relationship between psychology and Judaism.

The most significant study in this field has been the work of Moshe Spero, who maintains that *Halakhah* precedes human reality, in the form of an *a priori* theoretical structure. This *a priori* structure is the foundation of reality. This *Halakhic* reality determines an appropriate psychological reality for man. Through a *Halakhic* ontology, human behavior ensues. Spero diagrams this as follows:

Halakhic ontology model:

Given: *Halakhic a priori* forms   psychological needs

cross-cultural expression of such need

Halakhic expression

(Spero, 1980, pp. 14-30).

Spero's *Halakhic a priori* model presupposes specific human needs, and creates a means for fulfilling these human needs. The difficulty with Spero's approach is that, philosophically and psychologically, it views man exclusively as an object. The *Torah's* purpose, as derived from *Lifnim Mishurat Hadin* and *Imitatio Dei*, is that its entire teachings, normative as well as homilectical, will create the psycho-*Halakhic* man of conscience, which includes man-as-subject as well.

Since Spero discusses grief and bereavement as part of the resolution of experiencing a death in the family, this will serve as my example as well. Spero maintains that this *Halakhic a priori* form makes grief and mourning a possibility and substantiates the development of cross-cultural expressions of bereavement (Spero, 1980, 22–23). Specifically, the *Torah* addresses the concrete *halakhic* institutionalization of bereavement via the laws of mourning. "Cross-cultural expressions of bereavement, even though they may not manifest *Keriah* (rending one's garment) or other specific Jewish guidelines, retain this essential *halakhic* nature" (Spero, 1980, p. 22). What is inherent in *Keriah* is inherent in the human psychology of bereavement. This can be diagrammed as:

		cross-cultural expressions of guilt.
Given: *Halakhic a priori Aveilut* (mourning)	*need for catharsis*	
		Keriah, (rending one's garment).

Thus, a *Halakhic a priori* law is the blueprint of human nature.

But this *Halakhic a priori* model objectifies man, and does not allow for the subjective human experience. The psycho-*Halakhic* man of conscience incorporates the basic *Halakhic* guidelines of human behavior, and allows man to utilize these norms in a manner that will allow the subjective man to emerge as well. An example will clarify.

The Rabbis decreed that as part of the bereavement process, friends and relatives should comfort the mourner for seven days (*Talmud, Moed Katan,* 19a). Spero's *Halakhic a priori* model, as well as Rabbi Soloveitchik's *Halakhic* man, perform this commandment in a thorough and meticulous fashion, incorporating all the minutiae and details of this delicate *mitzvah* (commandment).

The psycho-*Halakhic* man of conscience looks not only at the individual mourner during the seven day period; he also realizes that the seven day period is only the basic guideline in providing comfort. The psycho-*Halakhic* man of conscience looks also at the bitter cold, isolated eighth day of mourning for which no specific commandment exists to comfort the mourner—but where the commandments of *Lifnim Mishurat Hadin* and *Imitatio Dei* clearly delineate an entirely different way of approaching the seven day period, that eighth day, and the entire year. The clear delineation of the various time-frames of mourning (seven days, thirty days, twelve months) sets guidelines not only for the mourner but also for the community, which must assist the mourner in gradually rejoining that community. It is this concept of conscience coupled with psychological sensitivity that creates the fusion of subject/object man of conscience, or the psycho-*Halakhic* man of conscience.

It is ironic that on occasion, a true understanding of indigenous *Torah* values can motivate one to violate a *Halakhic* norm. The *Talmud (Berahot*, 54a) interprets the verse "It is time to act for the Lord: they have made void your *Torah*" (*Psalms*, 119:126), as allowing for the temporary abolition of Jewish law for the fortification of Judaism. The psycho-*Halakhic* man of conscience calls for a response to concrete situations that may differ from the objective *Halakhah*. This approach can begin an entirely new investigation of psychology and Judaism, one based not on a *Halakhic a priori* model but on a psycho-*Halakhic* conscience model.

The ideal that emerges, then, is that the human condition is one of contemplation and spirituality. On the other hand, Judaism requires man to act. In spite of the existing tension, one aspect cannot exist without the other; nearness to God *obligates* man to take moral action. Even the joy of basking in the reflection of the Divine splendor is conditional upon moral conduct, and may be achieved by virtue of such conduct. Judaism speaks of nearness to God: "whom have I in heaven but Thee?, and besides Thee I desire none upon earth" (Ps. 73:25). Man yearns for proximity to God, and for distance from all things which hinder this proximity.

Only the *personal* God can be a *commanding* God. There are religious rituals whose observance is expressed by accepting the obligation to implement the precepts; and, on the other hand, there is prayer. There is content in prayer—man prays about *something*—but the essence of prayer is direct contact with God.

For the believer, religious truth is irrevocable. At the same time it is an individual truth, a personal faith. Notwithstanding the internal conviction it may arouse in the believer, it is in no way transferable. It is not empirically verifiable. Ultimately, its source is in the psyche.

V – Summary

1) Conscience is an integral part of Jewish law and thought, as manifested in the *Halakhic* concepts of *Imitatio Dei* and *Lifnim Mishurat Hadin*.

2) The predominant view of the *Halakhic* man consists of man exclusively as an object. It lacks the emphasis of man's other component of man-as-subject. Rabbi Soloveitchik's *Halakhic* man shows his creative heroism by negating self, and becoming subservient to the will of God. The prototype of the religious *Halakhic* man is Abraham's submissiveness in accepting the Divine decree to sacrifice his son, Isaac.

3) Dr. Moshe HaLevi Spero's paradigm model of the integration of psychology and Judaism utilizes an *a priori Halakhic* model. This model also views man as an object, without allowing man's experience of the world to affect this *a priori Halakhic* model. Theoretically, this *a priori Halakhic* model rests on an intimate knowledge of man's nature, so that all his future human needs can be guided and channeled by a predetermined construct. This model also does not include the unique nature of every man's subjectivity, and how he experiences the world as man-as-subject.

4) The concept of psycho-*Halakhic* man allows man-as-subject to coexist with man-as-object. This adds a dimension to Soloveitchik's and Spero's models. This new model allows for a fusion of a subject/object modality, in which man's subjective experience of his world is united with Divine objective law in creating a man of synthesis—man as an object and man as a subject.

5) The psycho-*Halakhic* man must be able to fuse this subject/object dichotomy based on his conscience. The element of conscience must attempt to understand the inner morality of the law at the present moment, in specific circumstances. Man's conscience must serve as a check-and-balance system in the fusion of man's subject/object elements. The psycho-*Halakhic* man of conscience is not submissive when such subservience runs contrary to his autonomous sense of ethics and morality. Neither does the psycho-*Halakhic* man of conscience follow dictates of situational ethics. The psycho-*Halakhic* man of conscience utilizes the objective *Halakhic* guidelines, and grapples with understanding the inner morality and ethics of that law. He experiences the presence of God even as he integrates the here and now. Man's conscience reconciles the object/subject dichotomy, allowing man to hear and experience the living God talking to him. In that way, the quintessential aspect of the *Torah, Imitatio Dei* and *Lifnim Mishurat Hadin* are fully implemented. This approach places the psycho-*Halakhic* man of conscience in a constant dynamic balance, in contrast to a static balance. As Alfred North Whitehead proclaimed, there is change in the midst of order, and order in the midst of change (Whitehead, 1929). It is this model that can be used to delineate a new approach to psychology and its relationship to Judaism.

References

Altmann, A. (Ed.). (1969). Saadya gaon *Three Jewish Philosophers*. New York: Atheneum.
Belkin, S. (1978). *The Philosophy of Purpose*. New York: Yeshiva University Press.
Berman, S. (1977, 1975). Lifnim mishurat hadin, *Journal of Jewish Studies*. Volume 26, pp. 86–104; Volume 28, pp. 181–193.
Birnbaum, P. (1949). *Daily Prayer Book*. New York: Hebrew Publishing Company.
Blidstein, G. (1975). *Honor thy Father and Mother*. New York: Ktav Publishing.
Borowitz, E.B. (1984). The autonomous jewish self, *Modern Judaism*. Volume 4, Number 1, Feb., pp. 39–57.
Encyclopaedia Judaica. (1971). Jerusalem: The MacMillan Company.
Encyclopedia of Religion & Ethics. (1952). Edinburgh: T. & T. Clark. Originally published 1926.
Falk, Z.W. (1981). *Law & Religion*. The jewish experience. Mesharim Publishers: Jerusalem.
Fox, M. (1979). The philosophical foundations of jewish ethics: some initial reflections, *The Second Annual Rabbi Louis Feinberg Memorial Lecture in Judaic Studies*. Cincinnati: University of Cincinnati.
Guttmann, J. (1976), Religion and knowledge. (Hebrew). Bergman, S.H., and Rotenstreich, N. (Eds.). Jerusalem: Magnes Press, The Hebrew University.
Guttmann, J. (1976). *On the Philosophy of Religion*. Jerusalem: Magnes Press, The Hebrew University.
Heineman, I. (1954). *Darchei Haagadah*. Jerusalem: Hebrew University Press.
Heller, A.L. (18th Century). *Kezot ha-Hoshen*. (1960). Jerusalem: Pardes.
Hirsch, S.R. (1978). *The Hirsch Sidur*. New York: Feldheim Publishers.
The Holy Scriptures (3 Vols.) (1982). Philadelphia: Jewish Publication Society.
Jung, C.G. (1973). *Answer to Job*. Princeton University Press. Originally published 1960.
Karo, J. (16th Century). *Shulhan Arukh* (10 Vols). 1965. New York: M.P. Press.
Kierkegaard, S. (1941). *Concluding Unscientific Postcript*. Princeton University Press: Princeton.
Knight, J.A. (1969). *Conscience and Guilt*. New York: Appleton–Century–Crofts, Meredith.
Laing, R.D. (1967). *The Politics of Experience*. New York: Pantheon.
Landman, L. (1969). Law and conscience: the jewish view, *Judaism*. 18, 1, pp. 17–30.
Leeuw, G.v.d. (1938). *Religion in Essence and Manifestation*. New York: Harper. Originally published 1933.
Leibowitz, I. (1979). *Yahadut, Am Yehudi, Umedinat Yisroel*. (Hebrew). Jerusalem: Schocken Books.
Lichtenstein, A. (1975). Does jewish tradition recognize an ethnic independent of halakha? *Modern Jewish Ethics*. Fox, M. (Editor). Ohio: Ohio State University Press.
Linzer, N. (1984). *The Jewish Family: Authority and Tradition in Modern Perspective*. Human Sciences Press: New York.
The Midrash (10 Vols.) (1961). H. Freedman and M. Simons (Eds.). London: Soncino Press.
Maimonides, M. (12th Century) (1962). *Mishneh Torah*. (6 Vols.) New York: M.P. Press.
Maimonides, M. (12th Century) (1963). *The Guide of the Perplexed*. S. Pines (translator). Chicago: The University of Chicago Press.
Nahmanides Commentary on the Torah (13th Century) (1975). Charles Chavel (Translator). New York: Shilo Publishing House.
Peck, S. (1979). *The Road Less Traveled*. New York: Touchstone Book. Simon and Schuster.
Poole, R. (1972). *Towards Deep Subjectivity*. Harper & Row: New York.
Random House Dictionary of the English Language. (1967). J. Stein (Ed.). New York: Random House.
Sartre, J.P. (1956). *Being and Nothingness*. New York: Philosophical Library.
Scholem, G.G. (1965). On the Kabbalah and its Symbolism. New York: Schocken Books.
Shilo, S. (1978). On one aspect of law and morals in jewish law: lifnim mishurat hadin, *Israel Law Review*. 13, pp. 359–390.

Sifra. In Malbim, M. (19th Century). Commentary to The Pentateuch: Leviticus (1964). New York: Grossman.
Soloveitchik, J.B. (1983). *Halakhic Man.* translated by Lawrence Kaplan. Philadelphia: Jewish Publication Society. Originally published 1944.
Spero, M.H. (1980). *Judaism and Psychology: Halakhic Perspectives.* New York: Ktav Publishing House and Yeshiva University Press.
Spero. M.H. (1985). The reality and the image of god in psychotherapy, American Journal of Psychotherapy. 39, 1, pp. 75–85.
Spero, S. (1983). *Morality, Halakhah and The Jewish Tradition.* New York: Ktav Publishing House and Yeshiva University Press.
The Talmud. (19 Vols.) (1961). I. Epstein (Ed.). London: Soncino Press.
Twersky, I. (1972). *A Maimonides Reader.* New York: Behrman House, Inc.
Twersky, I. (1980). *Introduction to the Code of Maimonides (Mishneh Torah).* Yale Judaica Series, Vol. 23. New Haven & London: Yale University Press.
Twersky, I. (1982). The *shulkhan aruk:* enduring code of jewish law, *Studies in Jewish Law and Philosophy.* New York: Ktav Publishing House, pp. 130–148. Reprinted from *Judaism 26*(1967), pp. 141–158.
Urbach, E.E. (1969). The Sages: Their Concepts and Beliefs. (Hebrew). Magnes Press, The Hebrew University: Jerusalem.
Whitehead, A.N. (1978). *Process & Reality.* Revised Edition. Free Press: New York. Originally published 1929.
Wyschogrod, M. (1981). Judaism and conscience, *Standing Before God.* Finkel, A., and Frizzell, L. (Eds.). New York: Ktav Publishing House.

Struggling With The Image of God

J. MARVIN SPIEGELMAN is a graduate in clinical and social psychology from UCLA (Ph.D. 1952) and of the C. G. Jung Institute in Zurich, Switzerland (1959). He has taught briefly at Hebrew University in Jerusalem (1958) and for seven plus years each at UCLA and USC. He has been in private practice in the Los Angeles area since 1959, and is the author of some forty articles and books, some in the area of connecting Jungian psychology with religion, Buddhism and Jungian Psychology, (with Mokusen Miyuki), is editor of a Modern Jew in Search of a Soul with twenty five authors, and Hinduism and Jungian Psychology with A. Vasavada. He has also published, in psychological fiction, The Tree: Tales in Psychomythology, Vol. 1 of a trilogy.

ABSTRACT: The issue of tradition versus autonomy in Judaism is discussed from a psychological point of view, particularly Jungian, in the context of the story of Jacob, his following of his mother's injunctions, which were also from God, his seemingly questionable qualities, his wrestle with the angel, and his redemption as an embrace of the opposites which are constellated when one has a direct experience of the Divine. Clinical examples and implications are drawn with the conclusion that conscience is the place where these opposites coalesce. It is shown that both orthodoxy and heterodoxy can meet in the embrace of the inner struggle.

When Rabbi Levi Meier, the Conference Coordinator invited my participation in this conference, he had tentatively entitled it *Tradition and Autonomy in Judaism*. My reflections on the theme of these psychological opposites led me to the conclusion that Conscience was one place where they met. I had planned to center my remarks on this when a reminder of the conference came to me with the title now transformed into *Conscience and Autonomy in Judaism*. I let the synchronicity stand as a validation of my conclusion, but now I saw that the implied conflict between collective and individual was being softened. All the better, then, that my theme of "struggling with the image of God" would continue the aspect of conflict, since there is, indeed, an implied possibility of opposition between these two aspects of religious life, without which creative innovation would be impossible.

So, then, my topic is the interplay of tradition and autonomy, one aspect of which can be seen as the "struggle with the image of God." By this I mean that every religion and every person has an image of God, conscious or unconscious, and that this image changes with time, experience and development. Every world religion, furthermore, has within itself significant elements which nourish both a collective and an individual encounter with the Divine. This would have to be true since we know, from a psychological point of view, that both dimensions are deeply imbedded in the nature of the psyche itself and constitute the fundamental basis upon which the individuation process proceeds. Without our general humanity and its particular expression in the traditions into which we are born, we are not even human. And without our personal uniqueness – a product of the concatenation of genes and environment, nature and nurture – that generality would be unremarkable. Religion, indeed, celebrates and dramatizes both aspects and provides a vehicle by which we can both recognize and participate in our morality via ritual and belief. It also gives us a structure in which our personal experiences of the Divine can be both evoked and meaningfully explained.

When all goes well, there is no breach between individual and collective, and a seamless web joins the two. This is true even when there is religious struggle, for example, between desire and the law. The resultant conflict, experienced by the person, can readily remain in the context of religious practice and eventuate in both deepened appreciation and more meaningful observance.

But what about when things do not go well? How is it when a person can no longer believe in or observe all the tenets of his or her faith, yet does not find himself/herself in rebellion? Or, even more to the point, what happens when a person has religious experiences, even experiences of God, which do not fit into the revealed expectations of the tradition? Is he/she to abandon these experiences as heretical? Should one – as is common – merely "demonize" these experiences as being outside of tradition and therefore false? Or can one struggle with these experiences, undergo within one's self the agonizing containment of the strife of the opposites, hoping and praying for the grace which will provide a solution?

As an example, in Buddhism, we are given the extraordinarily potent symbol of the Buddha sitting at the base of the Bo tree, asserting that he will not rise until he is enlightened, subjecting himself to all the gods and demons who assault him. The resultant way to enlightenment, as evidenced in the path of meditation, for example, can bring about an experience of the Self within. But does this realization in the ordinary meditator lead to individuation – particularity and uniqueness – or to another collective image of the "holy man"?

The latter distinction came home to me during my first analysis, when I was less than twenty five. I had come up against a brick wall of resistance in myself and, when I let this wall speak, following the method of Jung's active imagination, a short poem emerged in Biblical style.

Within this cryptic poem, was the following couplet:

> Holy man, hollow man
> Solo man, Soloman.

I understood this couplet to mean that the Holy Man was really a hollow man, in both senses of the word: empty, yet possibly pregnant in this emptiness, with a potential fullness of the Divine. The second line, however, suggested that the man who stood alone was the wise man, the Soloman. In short, the holy man was empty for me at that time, and I had to find my "holiness"—such as it was—from within my self. At other times, of course, I have had no such need, nor would I recommend this generally. Yet the distinction holds: we can find our religious figures both within ourselves and outside ourselves, and sometimes they are in conflict.

The truly religious person, however, is both encouraged to participate in this inner struggle and enjoined not to become heretical. And this is as it should be, since the collective force wants us to continue in it, to treasure its rich and soul-saving past, and to protect us all from the chaos of a nonbelieving world. These days we are all too clear about the dangers to civilization from those who have no religious commitment at all. But, unfortunately, we also see too clearly the dangers from those fanatics of religion who permit only one vision as the true one, and feel themselves obliged to convert others, and sometimes even condemn or kill those differently committed.

Now we must turn to our own religion, Judaism, and see how this conflict stands with us. In Judaism, we have no single great figure, but a series of comparatively human patriarchs and matriarchs who help us realize that God manifests in history and has a relationship with us, both passionate and particular, both collective and individual. There is, indeed, an image of Israel being married to God.

The great Dutch Protestant theologian, Gerhard van der Leeuw, has characterized our spirit not only as a religion of the covenant, but one in which there is unrest—unlike the religions of repose—and this unrest comes from the great Will of God Himself, moving forcefully and compellingly in history, realizing His own aims with us as a partner. Thus, more than with many others, ours is a religion of relationship (Leeuw, 1938, p. 709).

Among these patriarchs and matriarchs are the figures of Jacob and his mother, Rebekah. The former, who himself becomes Israel, is a central personality in this history, and, as such, is a crucial model for our theme.

The name Jacob means "one who takes by the heel, and thus tries to trip up or supplant" (Moss, 1963, p. 354). He buys his brother Esau's rights as a first born and also manages to receive his father's blessing as first born. This is hardly an auspicious beginning for a man destined to be the father of all the tribes of Israel! Yet he did this apparently questionable act by dutifully following his mother, Rebekah's, instruction. And she, in turn, was carefully carrying out what the Lord God Himself had told her. God was apparently going against His own rules. We remember that Rebekah was barren and Isaac entreated the Lord who promptly helped her to conceive. But twins struggled within her womb and she, herself, enquiring of God, was told that two nations struggled in her womb and that the elder would serve the younger. So, when Esau was the first of the twins to be born, followed by Jacob grasping at his heel, she knew that the younger would be her favorite.

We know the story of how Jacob, when found out, fled away from his wrathful brother Esau to his uncle's lands where he was sorely deceived. But even on his way to his uncle Laban, Jacob was visited by God when he slept at Beth-El, and was told that he would be blessed as the ancestor of a great nation. God would be with him, he was told. And Jacob then witnessed a great ladder ascending into heaven and the angels of God circulating up and down upon it.

Despite his seemingly questionable behavior, Jacob was chosen by God. We know, furthermore, that after Jacob suffered by the behavior of Laban, he went out rich and fruitful, but his own favorite wife, Rachel, initially suffered barrenness, and was herself a trickster. Ultimately Jacob made his peace with his uncle and returned, with wives, children and flocks, to the land that God had promised him. Fearful of his brother Esau's wrath, he sent gifts and also apologized to God, saying "I am not worthy of all the kindness and of all the truth which Thou hast shown unto thy servant" (Genesis, 32:11).

After this realization on his part (can we call it conscience?), Jacob had the memorable night in which he struggled with the angel of God, and held on until he was blessed. At break of day, he was blessed, and called the place Peniel, for he had seen God "face to face" and his life was preserved. After this, Jacob encountered Esau and he "bowed himself to the ground seven times." Esau embraced his brother and they both wept. The subsequent peace and mutual service was a fitting ending to a story which began not only with the birth of the warring brothers, but hints back to the conflict between Abel and Cain, and between Isaac and Ishmael. The brothers are reconciled and, finally, Jacob is once more rewarded with an appearance of God who changes his name from Jacob to Israel, from supplanter to "Perseverer with God."

This story is central in our connection on several grounds. First, we see a division in the human realm—the theme of the warring brothers and principles—hinting at a division in the Divine itself. Did not God reverse His previous pattern of blessing and birthright to the elder son? Did He not abet Rebekah's deception of her husband for His own aims? And why not, since this same God sorely tried his chosen one, Abraham, by ordering him to sacrifice this self-same son, Isaac! We have, here, an image of a God who, in mysterious ways, encourages man to change the effects of natural happenings even through questionable means (see the prophecy to Rebekah, Genesis, 25:23—and the elder shall serve the younger). The "plain man" and the shepherd take precedence over "hairy man" and hunter. Civilization and cultivation are to carry on the development of society beyond the hunting level of life. And even the idols, carried by Rachel, called "images," are allowed to be brought by her and buried by Jacob. We see in Jacob a powerful description of the struggle within man himself with his own dark side, abetted by the Divine. We glimpse the apparent multiplicity of tendencies within the unitary Godhead. It is from this that true conscience is forged.

But what do we mean by conscience? The eminent scholar at Hebrew University in Jerusalem, Zvi Werblowsky, asserts that "there is no Hebrew equivalent of our Western 'conscience'—not even an approximation" (1970, p. 81). Conscience is derived from the Latin *conscientia*, which means "knowing with" and implies a consciousness which is able to detach itself and enable the person to judge himself. Not so with the Jew, says Werblowsky. For Biblical man, to *be* was to *be addressed* by God. The Lord commanded and man obeyed. Rather, his response was to *hear* the command and obey. Disobedience meant not responding, shutting one's self off from God and from one's true being. The general implication throughout is that God's word is meant to be listened to, from outside of one's self, to effect "the heart" and, ultimately, when the Law is so imbedded on the inner man and "the heart" that they were one.

Werblowsky pursues this theme at length, showing that deep ethics and morality are not incompatible with a lack of the category of conscience as such, but imply a direct response to God or lack of it. For our purposes, we need only see in deeper measure that in Judaism the theme of struggling with one's conscience is a late development. Our main duty is only to be responsive to God. Once more, relationship is at the center.

How, then, are we to understand the statement by Jacob, quoted earlier, that he was "unworthy" of God's mercy and kindness? He was just very fearful of Esau's wrath. Or did it change? Can we not speculate that, in his anxiety, he turned away from the image of his brother's wrath to that of God Himself? Did not his experience of deception at the hands of Laban teach him something? R. Waddy Moss, scholar of the Hasting's Dictionary of the Bible is of that opinion: ". . . and what he needed supremely was not reconciliation with his brother, but the blessing of God" (Moss, 1963, p. 454).

We can only agree with this perception and add that *Jacob must have recognized that the supplanting of the "blessing" from his father was as nothing if he did not have the "blessing" of God.* And this was what he sought. He had already "had" it given to him, but now he had to "earn" it, or verify it. Once more, unimpaired relationship, despite previous gifts and promises, is the true "conscience" of the Biblical Jew.

Something similar is implied by the great Jewish scholar, Rabbi Joseph B. Soloveitchik, who, in his moving article, "The Lonely Man of Faith" shows that the man of faith is perforce lonely, that:

> It is God who wants the man of faith to oscillate between the faith community and the community of majesty, between being confronted by God in the cosmos and the intimate, immediate apprehension of God through the covenant, and who therefore willed that complete human redemption be unattainable (Soloveitchik, 1965, pp. 54–55).

The religious man, therefore, is not fully at home in community, and lives the dialectical role assigned to him. Psychologically, we would say that the man of faith, one who has a commitment to the Divine principle, perforce lives in a dialectical situation and, therefore, is in struggle. It is from this struggle that what we term conscience is derived, but *it is the Jewish contribution to see that the relationship is primary even though it is the law that is "commanded."*

Whatever it is that we mean by conscience, whether externally derived or inwardly achieved, it is clear that almost everyone has what might be called a "moral reaction." Jung (1970) has noted that this is part of nature itself. There is, within the psyche, a propensity to such considerations, even though the actual content of the moral reaction will change from culture to culture, time to time, and, indeed, during the course of an individual's development. The Eskimo, for example, can have a bad conscience when he has skinned an animal with an iron knife instead of the traditional flint one (Jung, 1970, p. 188), as well as feel twinges of guilt when he has left a friend in the lurch. In our Jewish tradition, the six-hundred thirteen commandments contain both such laws; the implication is that all of life, every aspect of behavior, is to be sanctified and governed by the law. In this sense it is moral.

Jung points out that:
Conscience is a psychic reaction which one can call *moral* because it al-

ways appears when the conscious mind leaves the path of custom, *mores*, or suddenly recollects it (Jung, 1970, pp. 199-200).

It is here that we see that "moral" behavior is linked with patterns and laws. When there is collision among them, or conflict with them, there begins to be the possibility of individual reflection and, therefore, *ethical* behavior can begin. The latter is possible only when there is conscious scrutiny, reflection about two different modes of moral behavior. An individual pattern emerges which can be called ethical rather than strictly moral. This ethic of serving God, even against the prevailing moral pattern, is apparent in Rebekah.

From a psychological point of view, one can say that such ethical considerations—here defined as requiring reflection and choice, arising out of struggle—produce higher consciousness. This, in turn, promotes new understanding and change in the divine images themselves. Such, I believe, was the experience of Jacob, when he demonstrated his own anxiety upon his return to Esau. He apparently knew that his struggle was with God Himself (when he says that he does not deserve mercy or kindness) but he is surely aware that his very questionable behavior was invited by God also. His perception gives us a hint of the much later experience of Job, who not only comprehended that God was beyond good and evil, but that a mortal could hold on to his own ethic yet not separate himself from God. This latter realization, I think, became possible as a profound development from what Jacob experienced, leading to a continuing change in our own images of the divine.

Jacob was given "the truth", face to face, he tells us, and Job saw the back of God. So seeing, he put his hand over his mouth and silenced himself. They both had a deepened understanding of the nature of the Divine image itself.

Jung has contributed an affecting discussion of the development of religious consciousness in his book, *Answer to Job*. In our present connection, I want only to point out that it is in this kind of conflict, in which psychic struggle occurs, including both collective patterns or *mores* and individual reflections, that consciousness grows. Tradition and autonomy collide in the soul of the individual and produce a truly *psychological* conscience that we can term ethics. By this we mean that the person has a hard-won personal standpoint, arising out of the struggle between what is "given" and what his own nature demands, and, at last, turns to his own images of the divine for a resolution. In this, his ethics become individual.

If we turn, now, to how these considerations appear in psychotherapuetic practice, in the rough-and-tumble of the struggle between autonomy and tradition, individual and collective, as it occurs in the painful reflections of people undergoing analysis, we are surprised.

The struggle between individual and collective, or for example between morality and desire, becomes manifest only when the person experiences guilt. And this guilt is by no means connected with religious considerations among most people who enter psychotherapy. Rather, we see that the psyches of most beginners on the psychological path of development are filled with all sorts of images and qualities which belong to past or historical religious attitudes but are not experienced as such by the person. How many drug addicts or alcoholics for example, realize that they are failed Dionysians, that they are in the grip of a god known well by the Greeks, but that they neither honor it nor struggle with it? How many atheists carry around within themselves a harsh and critical inner judge who condemns every deviation, however slight, from an attitude of rationalism and materialism? And how many pleasure-seekers are filled with the pagan lusts of Pan or the self-adornment of Aphrodite, without the religious attitude that the Greeks had, which made these experiences profound, blissful and in the service of culture?

In short, we find that the images and beliefs of old are carried around in the psyches of modern men, just as Rachel carried her old "images" when she accompanied Jacob. These, too, are "buried," just as Jacob's, but now in the unconscious and they emerge in people's dreams and fantasies as multiple tendencies toward experience and behavior. As people become aware of this inner diversity and potency, they learn that the demonization of parents and culture, of friend and foe, is a projection of their own inner "gods," named more banally as archetypes in our psychological jargon, and that their outer attitude of atheism or agnosticism, or even of belief in a particular religion, belies the true character of their own psyches.

In the work of therapy, people discover their own dark side, their shadows, as Jung called it, but also, in time, they discover the collective shadows and images that belong to us all. To continue with the process is to become more conscious and to take on the problem of uniting consciousness with the unconscious, and to both create and discover one's own ethic or way of being. In so doing, the individual becomes like Jacob himself, struggling with the angels—and demons—which present themselves in his/her psyche. One seeks a blessing, a harmony with the Divine or higher authority as it is discovered within one's self. The price we pay for this consciousness—and relationship—as with Jacob, is a deep wound. We are marked in the sinews. Jacob's way—as is the way of all the founding patriarchs and matriarchs—is that of individuation writ large, the collective individuation of an entire culture.

On our ordinary human level, such conflict is less heroic and more banal—fraught with daily frustration, the requirements of survival, and not so grand. The conscience that people discover, particularly if they are not in loving connection with a religious tradition, is usually harsh, mechanical and quite uninspired. The inner voice is simply uncaring, treats the person like a machine, or is equally condemning of others who do not do as the person wishes or this voice righteously demands. And, strangely, people succumb to this voice, not by obeying its commands, usually, but by often going against it, and then suffering its endless abuse. Surprisingly, if one considers the Freudian conception of the superego, for example, such a harshness was not generally experienced by the person in his own childhood. Rather, it seems that this collectively experienced moralizer is just the result of an image of "god", as one might call it, *who no longer has a true relationship to the ego*. It is a part soul gone bad. And patients usually find remarkable the suggestion that one could answer back to this inner voice and say to it, for example, "I am no mere machine. Why do you treat me so badly and without human regard?" It is as difficult to say "No" to such a tyrannical god as it is to say "No" to the other tyrannical gods of desire!

It is possible, however, to engage in a relationship with these diverse inner strivings and promptings and to acknowledge that one's psyche is the home for them, and the ego is an agent, or mediator, trying to reconcile these as best he/she can. When one takes on such a struggle— "struggling with the old images of god fallen into the unconscious" one might say—the outcome is true autonomy and individuality, which both honors tradition and the self. This, at deeper levels, is experienced as a religious struggle, and one's images of the divine itself perforce change.

I think, now, of a committed Hindu who, in the course of his analysis, rediscovered the rejected Christian aspects of himself, to say nothing of the pagan, and the process was one of discovering/creating a most individual religious attitude. I think, too, of several young Jews who had immersed themselves in various eastern religions and sects and finally had to come home to their own Jewishness. Not as the prodigal son, I hasten to add, since their apostasy and embrace of the alien was just as real as their return or *teshuva*, but they, too, had to find an individual way to the God that was discovered both in their own souls and revealed in the tradition into which they were born.

The foregoing examples sound a bit grand, I know, but they are, indeed, no whit different from the more frequent, ordinary and banal struggle that we all have with these archetypes within ourselves, whether interpreted as "remnants" or "vestiges" or experienced with the full power of the numinous. Some people can find their reconciliation within themselves without the long, hazardous path of the inner night-sea journey. Others need to find and live their own myth, their own story of relationship to the Divine. For those who can do this and remain within the sacred dimension of tradition, such as is described by Rabbi Soloveitchik, all the better. For those who cannot, they can comfort themselves with the possibility that the Divine is working in them, too, and that it seeks a particular realization and fulfillment which belongs to no one else in that unique way. In this struggle, whether within tradition or outside of it, we all succeed and we all fail, since we are always dealing with the *images* of the Divine which are manifested in us, and we know, as is revealed in Kabbalah, that the *Ain Soph*, God which lies beyond and transcends all images, is the One we finally serve. As with Jacob's vision of the circulating angels on the ladder to heaven, we work from manifestation to transcendence and the reverse. In this struggle, we honor what is revealed, what finds its home in our psyches. We are true inheritors of the Covenant, thereby, since we serve a never ending *relationship* with God as is discovered in tradition, in experience and in one's self.

As I was thinking of a clinical example of such a struggle between tradition and autonomy, with the resultant change in the image of God, what came to me was an incident in my own experience. Permit my clinical example to be myself. In 1966, a friend and I had a serious falling out with senior colleagues over our being elevated to the post of training analyst. Our belief was that our judges were unjust and unable to dialogue with us. They had equally negative opinions of us. One day, after a totally unfruitful attempt to dialogue with them, I realized that, in conscience, I had to resign from my loved and respected community of Jungians, since I could neither submit to their judgement nor convince them. Conscience led to aloneness.

As I drove home over the hill, weeping profusely over this loss and with my pain, I had a vision of two old men, grandfathers who came to me after the break with my spiritual fathers. One of these two was my actual grandfather, an orthodox Jew who died at the age of ninety seven. I visited him weekly during the first year of my analysis, back in 1950, the last one of his life. For me he represented all that was enduring and whole in our Jewish tradition. The second grandfather was C.G. Jung, whose work had absorbed me from the age of twenty four onward and who is, in my view, the leading spiritual figure of the twentieth century. These two, one a symbol of tradition, the other a symbol of individuation, came to me and embraced me. They laughed and drew me to them, and we all danced a *hora*. With this vision, I was able to go on, to project less on temporary collectives, such as societies, for my spiritual community, and to stand alone. It took me fourteen years, just like Jacob, to once again resume my membership in that society, and be less demanding of it.

More importantly, it took all those years for me to solidify my own uniqueness, and to creatively relate to a larger world than was represented to me in those earlier days. Like Jacob, I had to struggle with my own images of God, until I understood more "truth" and could also come to a place where I, too, could "bow seven times." In all those years, my own struggle was with the image of God, as revealed to me from inner depths, and I wrote several books mirroring that struggle (Spiegelman, 1974; 1982, in press).

So, I am deeply indebted to the figure of Jacob in our tradition, which, incidentally, was also the name of my grandfather and is one Hebrew name of my son, as well. For the pursuit of individuation, I am also indebted most profoundly to C.G. Jung, who wrote as follows:

> Individuation and collectivity are a pair of opposites, two divergent destinies. They are related to one another by guilt. The individual is obliged by the collective demands to purchase his individuation at the cost of an equivalent work for the benefit of society. So far as this is possible, individuation is possible (Jung, collected works, vol. 18, p. 452).

Finally, I need to remind myself of the acclamation of the *Shma* in our faith: we proclaim our commitment to God as One. Psychologically, in addition, we know that the One is "given" as a beginning, but also is a consequence of deep inner work. This Oneness, furthermore, surely makes possible a unity between tradition and autonomy.

References

The Bible. (1917). Philadelphia: Jewish Publication Society.
Jung, C.G. (1970). A psychological view of conscience, in *Conscience.* Various Hands, Edited by Curatorium of the C.G. Jung Institute, Zurich. Evanston: Northern University Press.
Jung, C.G. *The Symbolic Life.* Collected Works, Volume 18.
Leeuw, G.V.D. (1938). *Religion in Essence and Manifestation.* London: George Allen and Unwin. Originally published 1933.
Moss, R.W. (1963). Jacob, in *Hastings Dictionary of the Bible.* New York: Charles Scribner's Sons.
Soloveitchik, J.D. (1963). The lonely man of faith, *Tradition,* 7, 2.
Spiegelman, J.M. (1982). *The Tree: Tales in Psychomythology.* Phoenix: Falcon Press. Originally published 1974.
Spiegelman, J.M. (1984). *The Quest.* Phoenix: Falcon Press.
Spiegelman, J.M. (in press). *The Love.* Phoenix: Falcon Press.

Werblowsky, R.J.Z. (1970). The concept of conscience in jewish perspective, in *Conscience*, Various Hands, edited by the Curatorium, C.G. Jung Institute, Zurich. Evanston: Northwestern University Press.

New from Human Sciences Press

McKee, Patrick L., Ph.D., and Heta Kauppinen, Ph.D.
THE ART OF AGING
A Celebration of Old Age in Western Art

One hundred and fifteen works from the history of Western European art, in which the experience of aging is pictorially represented, demonstrate how artists have made vitally important contributions to our understanding of aging. Selected by leading authorities in the fields of gerontology and art education, these works, and commentaries provided by the authors, provide insights into the experience of aging that are unique to art. The works presented offer profound illumination of the experience of growing old, including life-style in old age, the achievement of wisdom, relationships between generations, and myths about aging.

1986　　　　　　　　208 (approx)
0-89885-304-4　　　　　　$24.95

Morrison, Morris R. Ph.D. editor
POETRY AS THERAPY
Foreword by Roger J. Williams Ph.D.

This interdisciplinary volume on the role of poetry as an agent in the therapeutic process presents articles by scholars in the fields of English and Italian studies, history, journalism, art, movement and drama, along with contributions from practitioners of psychiatry, psychology, counseling, rehabilitation and social studies. Together, they provide a unique perspective on the vast potential of poetry as a therapeutic tool which can break through the resistances of deeply troubled people, allowing them to communicate with their therapists in a much more meaningful dialogue.

1987　　　　　　　232 pp. (approx.)
0-89885-312-5　　　　　　　$29.95

 HUMAN SCIENCES PRESS, INC.　Phone orders: (212) 243-6000
72 FIFTH AVENUE　　　　　　(have credit card information ready)
NEW YORK, N.Y. 10011-8004